Using Information Technology

Marie Claire Williams

M. G. Mostfa

Student Handbook

Heinemann

Heinemann Educational Publishers,
Halley Court, Jordan Hill, Oxford OX2 8EJ
a division of Reed Educational & Professional Publishing Ltd

Heinemann is a registered trademark of Reed Educational & Professional Publishing Ltd

OXFORD   MELBOURNE   AUCKLAND   JOHANNESBURG   BLANTYRE
GABORONE   IBADAN   PORTSMOUTH NH (USA)   CHICAGO

First published 1997
Second edition published 2001

2004   2003   2002   2001   2001
10   9   8   7   6   5   4   3   2   1

A catalogue record for this book is available from the British Library on request.

ISBN 0 435 45144 8

Typeset by TechType, Abingdon, Oxon

Printed and bound in Great Britain by Biddles Ltd, Guildford and King's Lynn

Screen shots reproduced with permission from Microsoft Corporation

Tel: 01865 888058 www.heinemann.co.uk

Contents

Introduction

What is an NVQ?

An NVQ (National Vocational Qualification) is a standard that has been introduced throughout England and Wales specifically for work-based qualifications.

Assessment strategy

What is in the standards?

All NVQs consist of a number of *units*. A unit is a complete section of knowledge, e.g. how to use a computer and printer to produce documents to the satisfaction of your supervisor. Each unit is broken down into a number of *elements*, e.g. there are separate elements for entering the data, manipulating the data and printing the documents. Each element is described by a number of *performance criteria*. These spell out the things you have to do and the skills and knowledge you need to demonstrate, e.g. all the required data is entered and is done on time.

You are assessed against these standards and are required to demonstrate your competence for *all* the performance criteria and across a specified *range* (the scope and the variety) of activities.

Do you take an exam?

As this is a qualification to demonstrate your *skills* and *knowledge* for the workplace, you do **not** do exams but gather together evidence of your ability to do the work to an agreed set of standards. This evidence needs to be put together into a portfolio for assessment.

What form can the evidence take?

There are two main types of evidence: performance and supplementary.

1　Performance evidence results from doing the job and will consist of:
　　a　end products – e.g. plans, hard copy, disk files, etc.;
　　b　observation of activities – your tutor/assessor/supervisor will need to watch you carrying out some of the tasks that you include in your portfolio of evidence.
2　Supplementary evidence may include:
　　a　questions and answers (written and oral) – your tutor/assessor/ supervisor may sit down and ask you questions or may give you a worksheet to complete;

b   statements by yourself, supervisors and colleagues;

c   previous certificates of competence, e.g. CLAIT or word processing certificates.

As this is a vocational qualification, the *primary* or main sources of evidence of competence wherever possible should be from performance evidence, i.e. real work that you have done. For some elements, it is also possible for assessment to take place in a *realistic working environment* – this is one which reflects the expectations of industry and commerce by efficiently and effectively using *currently acceptable* information technology (IT).

Presentation of your portfolio

Your portfolio will need to include the recording systems required by the awarding body. For each item of evidence this will need to show:

- which *units*, *elements* and *performance* criteria it is evidence towards;
- who has assessed it; and
- when, where and under what conditions it was carried out.

You will need to compile an index and be able to cross-reference your documents.

As this NVQ is about working with new technology, you should be well equipped by the time you are completing your qualification to use many of the techniques of the software to enhance the presentation of your evidence.

The evidence you compile in your portfolio is assessed by an NVQ assessor and this assessment is confirmed by an internal verifier. An external verifier from the awarding body will also check a sample of the assessments.

Information about the structure of this NVQ

This NVQ is different from many others in two important ways. Firstly, much of the evidence to demonstrate that you are competent comes from the product, that is, the work you produce using the computer. This means that in some instances it may be possible to provide appropriate evidence in a 'realistic' rather than 'real' environment. Secondly, much of the evidence for the mandatory units will need to come from the optional units you choose to do. While this means that much of the evidence for one unit is also evidence for other units it also makes the recording, tracking and presentation of your completed portfolio more complex. However, this does mean that with a good index and clear cross-referencing of the contents of your portfolio, you can cut down on the total volume of evidence that you need to produce.

For this NVQ you are required to complete the four mandatory units and at least two of the five option units. This book contains information about all the units. The option units you choose may, to some extent, be restricted by the computing facilities that you have access to. If you are at work you are strongly advised to choose options where it is easy for you to provide evidence – something you are doing at work – not something completely different. You may find that you will need to negotiate additional training and computing opportunities outside your normal area of work to complete all the requirements of the qualification.

The mandatory units are primarily concerned with:

- best practice when working in the IT environment, including health and safety;
- developing and improving your own effectiveness in IT.

The optional units are concerned with:

- effective use of individual applications of IT.

Much of the evidence for the mandatory units can be provided through your work for the optional units you have chosen. For example, as you are producing documents using word processing software (Unit 202) you will also be carrying out the activities that are to be assessed in Unit 201 (Enable the Use of Information Technology) and Element 204.2 (Maintain your own file structures).

While a large part of the qualification is concerned with the application of information technology and the demonstrated practical use of computers to carry out specified activities, it is not possible to achieve this without a good understanding and working knowledge of the complete installed computer system, its components, peripherals and facilities. You can't choose the *best* way to do something if you don't know the choices open to you. It is also essential to be able to demonstrate knowledge and awareness of the relevant legislation, especially with regard to data protection, computer misuse, software copyright and health and safety.

Terminology

When you are studying for an NVQ, one of the first things you need to do is become familiar with the terminology that is used in the qualification. Included at the back of this book is a glossary of NVQ terminology. When a new term is first used it will be explained in the text. However, most people do not read textbooks from cover to cover, so if you come across a term you do not recognise or understand, have a look in the glossary before continuing.

Information technology itself has an ever-growing set of terminology which you also need to learn. This will be treated in the same way – that is, when a new term is used it will be fully explained in the text and will also be included in the IT glossary at the back of the book. The terminology of computing is often confusing at first. It is, however, an important part of this qualification that you become familiar and at ease with the language used. You will be better able to cope with new aspects of the technology as you meet them and will also be able to communicate with 'experts' and therefore less likely to make wrong choices about what to use or buy.

Data protection, copyright and computer misuse

This NVQ is about demonstrating that you can work effectively in an information technology working environment. To be able to do this you should have good knowledge and understanding of the importance of the data and the legislation and regulations that specifically relate to working in this type of situation.

Working with data

Computer systems for most users centre around the input, processing and output of data. Data is at the heart of the organisation. When working with data there are three main areas to consider:

- quality and accuracy;
- integrity; and
- data security.

Quality and accuracy

How often have you heard someone say 'The computer's got it wrong' or 'It's due to an input error'? As organisations, and indeed our lifestyles, become more and more dependent upon computer systems, these excuses become less acceptable. The methods of inputting and processing data are more sophisticated and more 'user friendly', and this should mean that the quality and accuracy of the data improve. Most desktop software packages have a range of built-in checking facilities such as spell checkers, but there is still considerable scope for mistakes to be made.

Case study: Duke's Designs

Claude Duke is concerned about the quality of some of the data that is entered into the computers in his business and needs some ideas on what can be done to improve the situation. Below are three fairly typical problems that have arisen in the past few weeks.

1 The company's financial statement has been sent out to the board with the data figures for June and July the wrong way round.

2 A spreadsheet has been produced showing next year's budget. Some revisions had been made the day after the initial input, but the earlier version has been sent out by mistake.

3 A work-experience trainee on placement from the USA has been working in the general office. She has extremely good word processing skills and has produced the 'copy' for the printers for next year's catalogue. However, the document uses US spellings.

Listed below are three simple, basic techniques for improving the quality and accuracy of data. Match the solutions to the problems.

a Use of a spell checker.

b Proof-reading before despatching.

c Using the automatic system date facility.

Integrity

Integrity of data refers to the correctness of the data throughout its life in the system. To ensure this, the following are needed:

1 **Adequate checks for validity and accuracy at point of entry**
   - *Verification of data* – this involves checks to make sure that the data is entered accurately. (For example, the data is entered twice into the computer by different people, the two versions are compared by the computer and any data with differences is rejected for checking and re-input.)
   - *Capture of appropriate data* – you should collect and store the data in the best way so that it will not need processing simply to keep it current. (For example, use date of birth rather than age, as the latter becomes incorrect as time goes by.)
   - *Batch totals* – these are particularly important when handling numeric, mainly financial, data. (For example, the total value of a set of invoices is calculated and entered at the start of the input process. As each invoice is input the computer keeps a running total of all of the invoices. When the complete set (batch) has been input the computer compares the input total with the calculated total and will only accept the batch if the totals match.)
   - *Validation of data* to make sure that it is an allowed value or response. (For example, the payroll system may be set up to accept only a range of values as no one has a salary above or below a limit; or to make sure that only the correct names of the departments can be entered, they are selected from a 'pick-list'.)
   - *Check digits* are extra digits, usually in an account number, which are based on the numbers in the account number and their sequence. If any number is entered incorrectly, or the numbers are entered in the wrong order, then the check digit will indicate that this is not a valid account number. (For example, your electricity or telephone

account number has an additional digit which ensures that if any one digit of the code is entered incorrectly, then it should be identified as an error *before* you get the bill! This doesn't mean that the bill is correct but it does mean that the bill is sent to the right person.)

- *On-screen checking* – that is, visual checking (proof-reading). (For example, when your account number is entered, your name is displayed on the screen for the operator to check before continuing with the rest of the input.)

2 **Adequate controls throughout processing to ensure that the data is not accidentally altered or destroyed during processing**

- *Control totals* are produced by the system at various stages of a process and should be checked manually as well as by the system to identify any errors or corruption of data. (For example, in a cheque printing system, during the first stage of the process which involves identifying those suppliers for whom cheques are to be printed, the total value of all cheques will be calculated together with the total number of cheques. This control information will be printed and also passed on to the next stage of the process. As the cheques are printed, a running total will be made of the values together with a count of the number of cheques. These second-process control totals will be compared by the computer at the end of the process but should also be printed for a manual check.)

- *Check sums* are similar to check digits and are used to ensure that the numbers and sequence of numbers are not corrupted as the data is passed from one process or system to another. (For example, all the retail outlets of a chain store send their sales data through a communications link to the head office every evening after close of business. A mathematical formula is applied to this numeric data and from this an additional item of data (the *check value*) is derived. When the data is sent to the central computer system this additional item is also sent. When the data is received the same formula is applied and the two check values are compared to make sure they are the same. If they are not, the receiving computer can send a message requesting that the data is sent again as there is apparently an error.)

- *Backup and recovery procedures* – see 'Housekeeping' in Unit 204 on page 53.

However, all that any of these systems can do is:

- reduce the likelihood of input errors by the operator;
- reduce the chances of internal, computer errors – the computer software is still only as good as the quality of the programs;
- reduce the probability of processes being omitted or forgotten, by working to agreed procedures; and

- alert the user to errors that are encountered so that they can be responded to.

No amount of computer validation and checking removes the responsibility for the integrity of the system from the operator, user and ultimately manager. When an error is identified, it needs to be acted upon.

An error might be simple and straightforward and within the immediate authority of the operator. For example, if an account code has been entered incorrectly (two digits might have been transposed – 12435 was entered instead of 12345) this can easily be rectified by re-entering the numbers in the correct sequence.

The error might have arisen, however, from outside your area of work or responsibility; it would be extremely unlikely that you would be authorised to decide what the correct data should be when entering data into the payroll system. If the value input for a new member of staff's salary has been rejected by the system as greater than expected (possibly because the annual salary has been put on the input document rather than the monthly amount), you would need to record this error and take it either to your line manager or possibly the person who authorised the original document.

Data security

Adequate controls are needed throughout systems to ensure only authorised access to the data. This can be achieved by the following:

- *Passwords* for systems, programs and data. (For example, where you use a computer at work your password will probably give access to the main set of programs such as the word processing and spreadsheet packages, but only if you work in the finance department can you also access the accounts system, and only if you are responsible for managing the department can you also access budget data.)
- The regular *changing* of user *passwords*. (For example, in most organisations the system will automatically prompt you after a set number of days to change your password.)
- *Communications controls* to ensure that only authorised people can connect to the computer from an external link. (For example, a system known as 'dial-back' is used by many organisations. When a user – such as a home worker or a worker based at another site – connects to the computer, the system knows from the user's log-in and password who he or she is and will have details of the authorised user's phone number. The link is immediately disconnected and the computer 'dials back' to the external system from which he or she will be connecting.)
- Access on a *need-to-know* basis – this means that access is denied to everyone unless they are positively identified as needing access to that system or data. (For example, the organisation may require that all password levels have to be requested in writing by the user with a

description of why he or she needs the data. This then has to be countersigned by the line manager.)

- Ensuring that visitors to areas where there are computer screens are not able to view the data. (For example, careful consideration needs to be given to the positioning of equipment, particularly in areas where access is not restricted; users need to follow procedures about exiting from software, particularly where sensitive data may otherwise be left visible on the screen.)

Case study: Duke's Designs

Zeena works in the accounts section, processing invoices and general accounts data. She is aware that a number of her colleagues 'share' passwords with each other. They do this mainly so that they can help each other out when there are tight deadlines to be met. However, Zeena is also aware of at least one *former* colleague who still visits occasionally and could still gain access to the system.

She is concerned about the potential for a breach of security but also aware that this situation must be handled carefully as regards her colleagues. She has decided that she must do something about this but would rather not get her colleagues into trouble unnecessarily.

It is clear that the main reason for this problem is that the organisation does not have an appropriate system or set of procedures. One answer would be to introduce a system that required all users to change their passwords regularly, e.g. every 20 days.

Write a memo for Zeena to send to her supervisor, tactfully putting forward this proposal, identifying *potential* weaknesses in the current system, without referring to the current practice of her colleagues.

The legislation relating to working with computers

The use of computers in all areas of work and leisure is growing rapidly. As a computer user, you need to know about the various aspects of legislation relating to working with computers. The main areas that you need to be particularly aware of are data protection, copyright issues and computer misuse. You also need to know about the health and safety requirements. This is covered in detail in Unit 206.

Data protection

What is meant by data protection and why is it necessary? More and more information about people is being stored on computers and more and more people have easier access to it:

- Worldwide communications systems are becoming more powerful by the day. It is now possible for data held almost anywhere in the world to be accessed rapidly in most other parts of the world.
- The speed and processing power of computers means that facts and figures about individuals are more likely to be analysed and brought together.
- The proliferation of computers in both business and the home means that almost anyone has access to this technology. As the cost of online access is reducing rapidly, this expansion will undoubtedly continue.

There are many advantages to this widespread computerised data access, but it brings with it the need to ensure that the data, and the individuals concerned, are protected. How many organisations do you think hold data about you in an electronic form?

Figure 1 shows the likely computerised record holders for most people in the UK today. The list is by no means complete, but is intended to highlight the extent of electronic collection and storage of personal data. Most of the time we are not made aware that this information is going to be held as a permanent record and we rarely think twice about supplying the details. Although data users are required to advise you that this information will be held, and to give you the opportunity to request that they do not make it available elsewhere, it is often in such small print that you don't notice it.

While most users record this data for entirely legitimate reasons, there are many organisations who 'sell on' mailing lists which frequently result in 'junk' mail and unsolicited sales approaches.

Go through the list in Figure 1 and see how many of these data users probably have data about you.

What is the legislation?

The legislation that needs to be considered includes (a) that which relates specifically to this country and is usually made by the passing of an Act of Parliament; and (b) the requirements of the European Union, which are usually set down as directives to which all member countries must then conform. The current British legislation is contained within the *1998 Data Protection Act* which replaces the 1984 Act. The 1984 Act was concerned with personal data – information about living, identifiable individuals, which is 'automatically processed'. The 1998 Act sets rules for processing personal information and applies to organised paper records as well as those held on computer.

It is based upon eight guiding principles:

- Data must be processed lawfully and fairly – this includes the requirement that the data has also been obtained fairly and lawfully and that the data subject has been notified of the intention to process the data.

Organisation	Type of data	Tick the ones that apply to you
Health authority	Personal details including name of GP	
GP	Medical history	
Local authority	Residential and possibly employment and benefit details	
Bank	Credit rating and history; some employment details	
Employer	Employment history; some medical records	
DVLC Swansea	Vehicle and driving licence details	
PNC	Vehicle details	
Inland Revenue	Tax and employment history	
Education authority	Education and some family details	
Insurance companies	Motor – motoring offences, driving details and history Life – health, employment, family details Home – home security, value of possessions	
Credit card and hire purchase companies	Credit rating, income, expenditure, lifestyle	
Societies and organisations, e.g. AA, RAC, Reader's Digest, etc.	Limited but tend to have lifestyle details	
Large retail outlets where you have used a credit card	Basic personal details plus details of purchasing history	

Figure 1 *Computerised record holders. Are there any others that you can think of? Add them to the list*

- Data must be held only for specified purposes – these have to be identified at registration.
- Data must be adequate, relevant and not excessive – the amount of data held should be the minimum necessary to meet the specified purposes.
- Data must be accurate and kept up to date.
- Data must not be held for longer than is necessary.
- Data subjects should be able to access their data and, where appropriate, have it corrected or deleted.
- Security systems must exist to ensure that unauthorised users cannot access, process, alter, destroy or disclose data.
- Data must not be transferred to a country outside the European Economic Area, unless that country has a similar level of protection for the rights of data subjects.

How does the Data Protection Act work?

The main operational aspects of this Act are the requirements on all data controllers (the people within organisations who determine how and why data is to be processed) to:

- notify the details of the types of data they hold and for what purposes;
- ensure that their systems have adequate controls to maintain the integrity of the data;

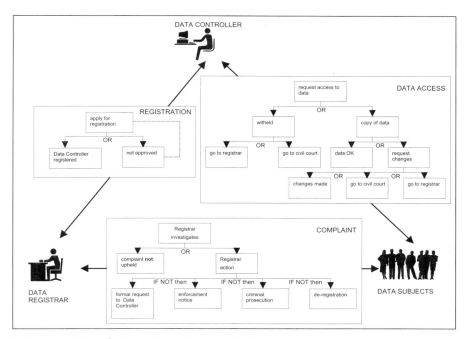

Figure 2 *How the Data Protection Act 1998 operates*

- ensure that they have adequate security on their systems to safeguard against unauthorised access; and
- set up procedures to enable the data subject access to his or her data and to have corrected any inaccuracies, unnecessary records or misuse (see Figure 2).

There is no requirement to notify manual records covered by the Data Protection Act, although they may be notified voluntarily.

The process of notification can be carried out either using the Internet, completing an online form, or by telephone when a draft notification form is completed based on the information provided during the conversation and is then sent for confirmation.

Case study: Laitwood Medical Centre

The GPs in this well-established medical practice have recently had installed a small network of computers to run their patient records and administration system so that they can be more responsive to the needs of their patients.

The practice manager has contacted the Data Protection Registrar and has received all the details about the legislation, the forms to register as a data user and the fees charged. She now has to supply the following:

- the name and address of the data controller;
- a description of the personal data to be held and of the purpose or purposes for which the data is to be held or used;
- a description of the source or sources from which the medical centre intends or may wish to obtain the data;
- a description of any person or persons to whom the centre intends or may wish to disclose the data;
- the names or a description of any countries or territories outside the UK to which the centre intends or may wish directly or indirectly to transfer the data; and
- one or more addresses for the receipt of requests from data subjects for access to the data.

Using this information, carry out the following tasks:

1 Create a table with three columns. In the first column, make a list of all the items of personal data that you think the medical centre might want to keep on its computer system.
2 In the second column, enter the sources of each item of data, i.e. who will supply the data.
3 In the third column, enter against each data item the people or organisations to whom the data may be disclosed.

Discuss what you have put into this table with your tutor.

The Data Protection Register, which contains the details supplied by the data controllers, is a public document maintained by the Data Protection Commissioner. A copy should be available in major public libraries and you can carry out a search on the Internet web site: www.dataprotection.gov.uk

CHECK IT YOURSELF

In most organisations there will be a person who is responsible for all matters connected with this legislation – the data controller. Find out the name and job title of the person who has this responsibility in your organisation. Enter this information in section 1 of the legislation checklist on page 20. You may also be able to get a copy of the details of the organisation's registration. If you can, include this in your portfolio of evidence.

Having identified and registered details of the personal data that are to be held, the data controller then needs to make sure that systems are set up to ensure the quality, accuracy and integrity of the data.

CHECK IT YOURSELF

What controls exist on the systems you work on? Find at least two examples for all three aspects of data integrity identified on page 4 and enter the information on the legislation checklist on page 20.

Are there procedures in your organisation for handling breaches or potential breaches of security? To whom would you report your concerns, and how? Are there any instances that you might have authority to deal with, and what would you do? Write a brief description and draft a memo to report this to the appropriate authority. Include this in your evidence folder.

The legislation is designed to stop the storage of 'unnecessary' personal data. No data controller should be holding personal data without good reason, nor should data be kept for longer than is necessary. When data controllers register, they are required to specify the purpose for which they are holding the data. As a data subject you may challenge this and have the data deleted if you can demonstrate that there is no legitimate reason for keeping it, but first you need to be able to see exactly what is held.

The data subjects – the people whom the data relates to – can request access to most data to check that the information is accurate and held for legitimate purposes. All registered data controllers are required to have a procedure for data subjects to gain access to their data.

The practice manager needs to set up a procedure for data subjects to request access to their data. The Data Protection Act specifies the following:

- the organisation can charge a fee for providing the access. It is currently set at a *maximum* of £10 for each category of registration.

- The request for access needs to be in writing.

- The organisation must obtain satisfactory proof of identity before disclosing any details.

- The data must be supplied, once all the above have been met, within 40 days.

The practice manager has decided that a leaflet is needed to explain the procedure.

Assuming that the centre provides a form for people to fill in to make their request, produce a simple, clear leaflet to tell people what information they can find out and how to do this.

CHECK IT YOURSELF

What are the procedures in the organisation where you are working? Is there a standard form to be completed? Ask for a copy of it to keep in your portfolio. Does the organisation charge an administration fee, and if so how much? Enter this information in section of 1 of the legislation checklist on page 20.

Breaches of the data protection legislation

What should you do if you become aware of a breach in the legislation? First, you need to make sure you are familiar with the procedures within your organisation for dealing with this situation. Although you are fully aware of the requirements of the law, your colleagues and your supervisor may not know the details. As the 'expert', and a responsible employee, you should advise them of the situation whenever necessary. This should be done as tactfully as possible, drawing their attention to the organisation's procedures for ensuring compliance with the legislation and dealing with any breaches.

Copyright

Copyright is about the ownership of rights in printed and recorded materials and software. It restricts what you are allowed to copy, how many times and for what purposes. The contents of this book are covered by copyright law.

The author and publishers had to make sure that the words and images did not 'belong' to anyone else. The copyright of this book belongs to the author. If you wish to use something that belongs to someone else, you must seek permission, acknowledge their copyright and, usually, pay to be allowed to use it. If you don't, it is the same as stealing.

There are two different areas of concern regarding copyright and IT. One relates to software and the conditions under which you are permitted to use it and the other is about the use of data, images and text which are held in digital form.

Software

Software is very costly to produce and very easy to copy. When you acquire an item of software you do not usually own the software – what you have purchased is a licence to use it. There are many different types of licences and it is always important to read the small print to make sure you are aware of what you can and cannot do. The licence could be any one of the following:

- *Single-user licence.* You may use this software on one computer only – the licence is usually for the user, who may transfer the software from one machine to another as long as it can be used on only one machine at any time.
- *Multi-user licence.* You may have up to an agreed number of users with access to this software – this may be by installation on a set number of computers, or it could be for specified numbers with network access.
- *Site licence.* You may be licensed to use the software for all the users on a site – some software providers consider a site to mean a physical location, while others interpret it more loosely and it could mean a whole organisation.
- *Machine licence.* Sometimes the software licence is attached to a particular computer rather than the user – in this instance you cannot transfer the software to a different computer without the permission of the copyright holder.
- *Server licence.* On a network, the licence may be restricted, like a machine licence, to a particular network server.
- *Network licence.* In a network environment you may have a licence for software to be used across the whole network – again there may be several different ways in which the term 'network' is interpreted. Most network systems software will be licensed under a network licence.

CHECK IT YOURSELF

Who is responsible for ensuring that adequate licences exist for the software that you work with? What is his or her job title? Is there a central record of software licences? If so, where is it held? Enter these details in section 2 of the legislation checklist on page 20.

It is illegal to copy and use software in a way that has not been licensed. It is extremely unlikely that anyone working in an IT department would ask you to do this. It is, however, possible that someone who doesn't understand copyright could ask you, e.g. a person who has some software on a computer at home and would like to use at work. If this happens, you should politely explain the law and consult your supervisor.

Some software is provided on a different basis, such as *shareware* and *freeware*. This is often software that has not been developed by a commercial organisation and therefore there is not the same concern about loss of income through unauthorised copying.

Shareware software is usually freely distributed in an unsupported form. It will usually come with details of how you can pay a nominal charge which will entitle you to patches (corrections), add-ons (enhanced features) and updates.

Freeware is software for which there is no charge, and can be freely distributed and used. This sort of software is not usually a full-feature application but often consists of a number of utilities and useful routines. This may be distributed through CD-ROMs attached to magazines, etc., or could be available on the Internet.

Data, images and text

In recent years the development of technologies that enable data, images and text to be readily captured and held in digital form has considerably increased concern about copyright. All the aspects of copyright in the print world now also apply in the digital world, but are more complex and potentially more difficult to control.

Scanners and software which not only capture images and store them electronically but have the capability to convert scanned text pages into text characters that can then be manipulated through word processors, etc. are now very cheaply and readily available. Access to the Internet, and the ability freely to download information in any form, provides a major potential source of information. This means that large quantities of words can be rapidly stored, altered and transmitted across networks. It also means that in the course of your everyday work, it would be easy to reproduce text and images belonging to someone else, without considering the fact that you are breaching copyright regulations.

Computer misuse

A whole range of activities can be considered under the term misuse. The *Computer Misuse Act 1995* identified three types of crime: breaking in; breaking in with further criminal intent; and alteration of data and programs.

Breaking in

The act of breaking into a computer system (hacking) is in itself a crime. It is also the first stage of doing damage to the system. Employees' carelessness with passwords is a common cause of unauthorised access. Also, particularly in a system where there are a great many users and passwords, hackers can find out passwords by trial and error. Too many people choose 'obvious' character combinations for their passwords, such as their date of birth, the name of a friend or member of the family. To a skilled and determined hacker these are their first choices when attempting a break in.

Breaking in with further criminal intent

If someone hacks into a system for reasons other than simply to do it, then they have committed a further crime. With the increasing use of computers for design purposes, many product plans may be vulnerable to theft through unauthorised access by competitors. Valuable customer details and company 'secrets' can be stolen and sold to competitors for profit.

Alteration of data and programs

Once inside the computer system the hacker, or other unauthorised user, may gain access to sensitive data. Employees and others from outside the organisation may alter data for their own benefit. Changes may be made to an employee's payroll data so that he or she is 'overpaid'; accounts receivable entries may be wiped out so that a customer is not charged for goods received; or accounts and charges in an accounts payable system may be set up so that customers are charged (and possibly pay) for goods or services they never receive. Finally, there is the possibility of wilful destruction of an entire database; this can be guarded against by the operation of regular and comprehensive backup procedures.

Sometimes a minor change to a program can enable someone to profit fraudulently. There have been a number of examples where employees have transferred the 'rounded down' fractions of amounts of money to their own or fictitious accounts and have succeeded, over several years, in committing significant thefts.

Theft of computer time

Many people use their access to their employer's computers to carry out their own activities. It is not at all uncommon for employees to word process the occasional personal letter, or to prepare their CVs to help them apply for new jobs. These activities are rarely considered to be a major problem although they are still a misuse of the computer system. However, there are many instances of employees using their employer's computer system to carry out activities for which they are being paid by others. In many organisations this would be treated as a disciplinary offence for which you could be dismissed.

What can organisations do to combat these activities?

Many organisations are reluctant to report or publicise the extent to which some of these activities take place because of the damage it could do to their credibility. Most organisations will have some level of security for access to the buildings, the staff work areas (particularly if it is a place that is open to the general public) and the computer systems (mainly through passwords, location of equipment, etc.). However, much of this crime is brought about through failure to follow procedures. How easy is it to 'talk your way in' to the building where you work or study, or walk in unchallenged? How secure are your passwords? What procedures exist for handling confidential information? What should you do if you become aware of breaches of security or misuse?

CHECK IT YOURSELF

Produce a brief, word processed report on the security systems in your organisation (this could be where you work, or at college). This will include information about getting into the building as an employee/student, arrangements for visitors and areas open to the general public. Describe the procedures for access to the computer systems, both physical security and passwords. If possible, include an example of a breach of security and how it was dealt with.

Legislation checklist

Section 1: data protection	
Name of person with responsibility	
Job title	
Is there a standard form?	Yes ☐ No ☐
Administration fee?	£
Systems to ensure integrity of data:	

1   Checks at data entry

2   Controls during processing

3   Control of access

Section 2: Copyright	
Name of person with responsibility	
Job title	
Is there a central register of licences?	Yes ☐ No ☐
If yes, where is it kept?	
Licence information:	
Application	
Type of licence	
Application	
Type of licence	
Application	
Type of licence	

MANDATORY UNITS

Unit 201 Enable the Use of Information Technology

This unit contains three elements:

201.1 Prepare for the use of IT
201.2 Follow procedures when using IT
201.3 Conclude the use of IT.

You need to demonstrate that you can carry out the routine operations necessary to make possible the use of information technology when carrying out your work duties.

To meet the requirements of this unit, you should have a good basic understanding of the range of hardware and software available to you. You should know how to start up and close down both the equipment and the software. You will also need to be familiar with the electronic storage of data.

Computer basics

The personal computer

Although it is in no way a requirement that this qualification is gained using a personal computer (PC), it is likely that the majority of candidates will do so. This computer may be operating as a stand-alone (single) computer or might be part of a network. For much of the qualification, and indeed for the majority of users, for most of the time this is not important.

You will be using a wide range of different application packages, usually decided by company or department policy. Again, it should not make any difference to your work for this qualification as long as the particular set up is capable of offering you the opportunity to carry out the required activities. It is not a requirement that you produce all your evidence using the same equipment or software. What is important is that you know what equipment you are working with and are aware of which packages and versions of the software you are using.

The first thing you need to do is find out some technical information about your working environment, often referred to as the specification. In order to do this you will need to complete the computer specification checklist on page 39. The following explanation will take you through the main components of the computer and discuss the terminology.

Main components of the computer: hardware

Processor

This is the part of the computer that carries out all the instructions, and is often described in the model number; part of the description will include some information about its speed. For example, you may be using a 486 66Mhz or perhaps a Pentium III 500Mhz machine. As models and speeds of processors change so frequently, you need to find out what is considered to be the current 'entry level' model. Computer magazines are a good source of such information.

CHECK IT YOURSELF

What is the make, model, processor and speed of the computer you will be using most frequently? Enter this information in section 1 of the computer specification checklist on page 39.

Memory

There are various parts of memory within a computer, each of which carries out a different function. The part that you, the user, need to be most aware of is called RAM (random access memory). This is the part of the computer that temporarily holds the programs and instructions you are using and the data that you are inputting. This part of the computer's memory is usually 'volatile', that is, when you switch the computer off anything that has not been stored will be lost.

Bytes

A unique unit of measurement is used for counting the size of various parts of a computer. This unit is called a byte. A byte is, generally speaking, the computer space necessary to hold a single character or code. Most of the time when describing the size of a component of the computer, you need to be talking in terms of thousands, millions and even thousands of millions of bytes. There are therefore a number of terms to describe these multiples. However, as computers are electronic and work in ons and offs, a different number base is used for counting – the binary system. The first multiple used is a kilobyte (Kb). 1Kb = 1024 bytes but this is usually referred to as one thousand. The next multiple is a megabyte (Mb). 1Mb = 1,048,576 bytes (1024 × 1024) but this is usually referred to as one million. The third level of unit is the gigabyte (Gb). 1Gb = 1,073,741,824 bytes but this is usually referred to as one thousand million, an American billion. For most PCs, the size of the RAM is expressed in megabytes.

CHECK IT YOURSELF

What is the size of the RAM in your computer? Enter the answer on the computer specification checklist on page 39.

Storage

One of the important reasons for using a computer is that you can store data and programs so that you can retrieve (recall) and amend them later. To do this you need to have a storage system. Most PCs will have two types of storage – a hard disk and a floppy disk drive.

The hard disk is the main, high-capacity disk which is usually permanently inside your computer. On this disk are stored all the programs and packages necessary to make your computer work, and you may also use it to store some of the data you wish to keep. The disk has a large capacity and is usually measured in gigabytes. Some computers, when connected to a network (see below), do not have their own hard disk drive but share the central resources.

The floppy disk drive has a much smaller capacity, usually 1.44Mb, and this disk is not kept permanently inside the computer but is removed when not in use. This means that you can use different disks to store different sets of data. We will look at the organisation of disks in the next unit.

CHECK IT YOURSELF

What is the size of the hard disk (if any) in your computer? How many floppy disk drives do you have? Enter this information on the computer specification checklist on page 39.

Peripherals

This is the term used to describe all the parts that are added to the computer – that is, they are outside the computer and are plugged into ports (sockets) in the computer. There may be a wide variety of different peripherals attached to your computer depending on what it is used for. The most likely ones are described below (see Figure 3).

Input devices

Keyboard

This is one of the main input devices and probably needs little explanation. However, it is important to note that there are some special keys on a computer keyboard.

There will be a Control (Ctrl) key and often there are two of these, just as there are two shift keys. They are both used for the same purpose, but it is convenient to have one on each side of the keyboard. The control is similar in concept and use to a shift key: it is used together with another key to send a different code to the computer. Then there is the Alternate (Alt) key which is another modifying key, like the shift and control keys.

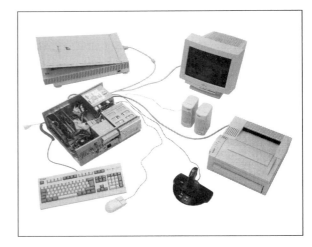

Figure 3 *Identify the peripherals in this computer system*

Across the top of the keyboard you will find a set of function keys (F1-F12); these are used in different ways by different packages and programs. There is also the Escape (Esc) key which again is used in different ways by different programs, but is frequently used to cancel an action.

Many keyboards have a numeric keypad on the right-hand side and also a set of cursor control keys. This keyboard is known as an extended or 102-key keyboard.

CHECK IT YOURSELF

Check what sort of keyboard you have and tick the box on the computer specification checklist on page 39.

Mouse

Most computers also have a mouse as an input device. This will have one, two or three buttons and has a ball underneath which is moved across a flat surface to control a pointer on the screen. Using a mouse effectively is a skill in itself and one that you need to acquire.

Do you have a mouse attached to your computer? How many buttons does it have? Enter this information on the computer specification checklist on page 39.

Output devices

VDU

One of the output devices you will have is a VDU (visual display unit). This might also be referred to as a monitor or screen – they all mean the same thing. This is used to enable the computer to communicate with you; what you input and the responses from the system appear on this device.

The VDU you are using will probably display a range of colours but can also be monochrome (black and white, green and black or amber and black). The quality of the display is described in terms such as VGA (video graphics array), SVGA (super VGA) or similar. To get high-quality graphics you will also need to have a video card with 4Mb of memory and an Advanced Graphic Port (AGP) inside the computer.

Do you have a colour VDU? Find out the quality of your monitor and enter this information on the computer specification checklist on page 39.

Printer

Printing is still the most frequently used form of permanent output. You will probably have a printer either attached directly to your computer or, particularly if you are working on a network, one available for you to use but shared with other computers.

The technology of printing is developing almost as quickly as that of the rest of the computer. Most local printers (not on a network) attached to PCs are either laser printers or ink-jet printers. We will deal in detail later on with the technology of the different types of printers. For now, it will be sufficient for you to find out what type of printer you have and the speed it prints at. If it is a laser or ink-jet printer, the speed is measured in pages per minute (ppm). If you have another type of printer, the speed may be measured in characters per second (cps).

What type of printer do you use? What is the make, model and speed? Can it print in colour as well as black on white? Enter this information in section 2 of the computer specification checklist on page 39.

Other peripherals

There may be a number of other peripherals attached to your computer, as there are many other types of input, output and storage devices. Some of the more frequently encountered ones include the following.

Storage

A CD-ROM is a compact disk which is capable of holding high volumes of data (approximately 650Mb) – this can only be written on once and is therefore not appropriate for data that needs to change. The speed with which data can be accessed, however, is about ten times slower than from a hard disk. There are now both write-once CD-Rs and rewritable CD-RWs; these are, however, significantly slower than a CD-ROM. CD-ROMs are often used to supply software, games and reference material (see Figure 4).

Digital Versatile Disks (DVDs) are a development of the CD. Unlike a CD, both sides can be recorded on and they can also have two layers. This, together with a much greater recording density, means that up to 17Gb of data can be stored. DVD recorders do exist, but are very expensive, so most drives are read only.

Figure 4 *Loading a CD-Rom into the disk drive*

Input devices

- *Light pen.* A pen-shaped input device which is pointed at the screen to make selections or to create images.
- *Scanner.* An input device used to capture images and text from the printed page.
- *Graphics tablet.* A flat board connected to the computer on which you can draw with a special pen or 'puck' images which are displayed directly on the VDU and can be stored in the computer.
- *Digitiser.* A generic name for an input device used for converting data in its current form into digital data which can be processed by the computer; a scanner is a digitiser; a graphics tablet can be used as a digitiser.

Output devices

- *Sound card.* A circuit board which enables high-quality sound to be produced on the computer – essential when using multimedia software.

- *Plotter.* An output device used to produce high-quality graphics data – the image is created using a number of different coloured pens which are picked up and put down by an 'arm' which moves across the paper. This type of printing is often used for CAD (computer-aided design) applications.

CHECK IT YOURSELF

Find out what other equipment is attached to your computer and enter the details in section 3 of the computer specification checklist on page 39.

Main components of the computer: software

Having identified the hardware that you use, it is equally if not more important to find out the specification of the software. There are two types of software – systems and applications.

You are now going to find out about the software that you use and record this information on a software specification checklist given on page 40.

Operating system

This is the set of instructions and rules which make the computer work. The operating system enables the computer to interpret each key you press, display the character it represents on the screen and make sense of it. It is necessary for the computer to be able to start up, to carry out your instructions and those of the software that you use, to save the work you do and to communicate with any attachments to your system such as disk drives, printers, plotters or devices to communicate with other computers.

The basic part of the operating system, the part necessary to start up the computer, is held permanently inside the computer in ROM (Read Only Memory). This is a part of memory you can only read from – you cannot change it by adding, editing or deleting anything. The rest of the operating system is normally held on the hard disk inside your computer. As new peripherals are added to your computer system, you will need to provide operating system software to let your computer communicate with these devices.

An additional part of an operating system allows you to carry out utilities – these are activities which enable you to use the computer more effectively and to keep it in order (e.g. making copies of files, deleting work that is no longer needed or moving files from one storage device to another). This type of activity is often referred to as 'housekeeping'.

When you buy a new computer, it may be necessary to install (set up) these parts of the operating system, but it is a simple and straightforward procedure which is mainly carried out by following instructions on the screen and responding to prompts for information. It is important to know which operating system you are using and which version number.

In recent years, computers have been made more accessible to general users by the introduction of user-friendly 'environments'. This is done by hiding the 'raw' operating system from the user and letting him or her carry out many of the basic functions through the use of *WIMPs* (**W**indows, **I**cons, **M**enus and **P**ointers) (see Figure 5).

CHECK IT YOURSELF

What operating system do you have on the computer you usually work on? You need to find out the name of the company who supply it and what it is called. What version number are you using at the moment? Enter this information in section 1 of the software specification checklist on page 40.

For most computer users, the 'environment' they work in is called 'Windows', but there are several other similar environments available. For example, on the Apple Macintosh, Apple OS (the operating system) is always presented to the user as an 'environment'. The latest versions of Windows (98 and 2000) are deemed to be a complete operating system.

CHECK IT YOURSELF

Do you use an 'environment'? What is it called? Find out what version number you are using and enter this information in section 1 of the software specification checklist on page 40.

Networks

Although many people use their computer as a 'stand-alone' PC, it is very common, particularly in the workplace, for a number of PCs to be linked together to work as part of a network. There are many advantages to networking, including the following:

- The users on the networked PCs can communicate with each other.
- It will often only be necessary to have one copy of the software stored centrally which all the users can access – but see the section on licences (page 16).

WIMPS	Examples
A *window* is an opening on your screen which lets you view an activity. You can have more than one window open at any time and can therefore look at and work on a number of different activities at the same time.	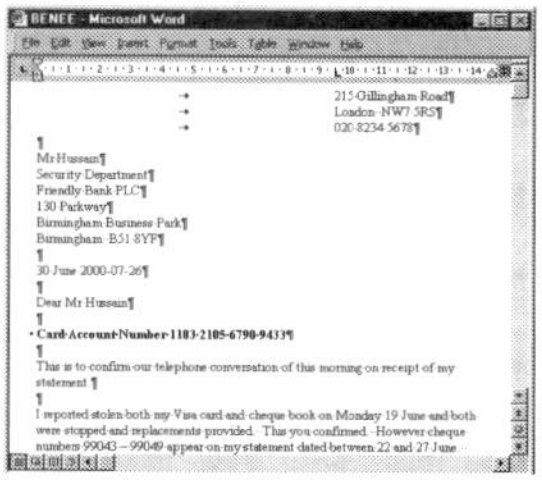
An *icon* is an image which is used to represent a command or function that you wish to carry out.	✂ cut 🖨 print 📁 directory or folder
A *menu* (drop down or pull down) is a set of options, usually used to give you a choice from a selection of similar commands or functions.	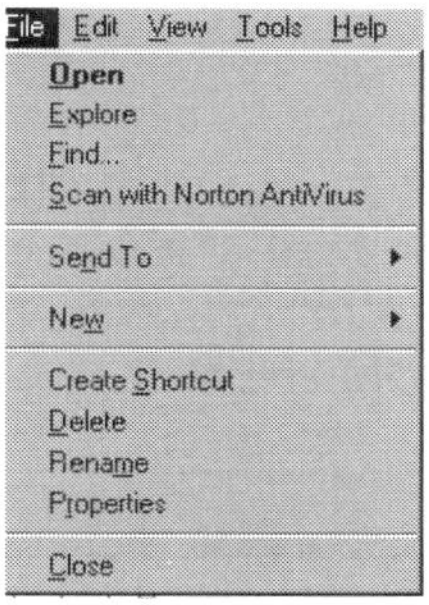
Pointers are the devices, such as a mouse or a light pen, that enable you more easily to use this environment. You do not need to be able to use the keyboard to issue commands to the computer as you can select the icons and menus using a pointing device, although for many functions this is slower than using the keyboard. As you become more proficient you may prefer to use the keyboard for some functions rather than pointing at icons and menus. *Pointer* is also used to describe the shape that moves around the screen as you move the pointing device.	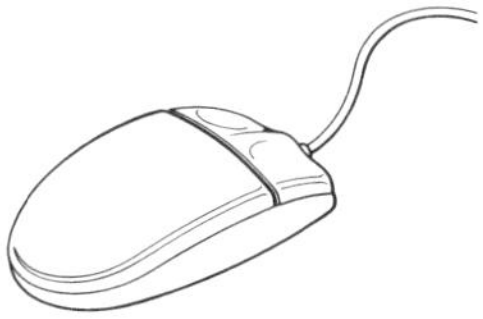 mouse 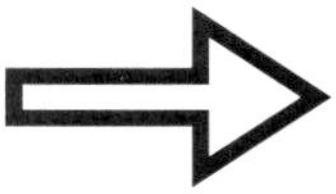

Figure 5 *Facilities to help you operate your computer more easily*

- Peripherals, such as printers, can be shared by a number of users, thus making better use of resources.
- Fast, high-volume data storage systems can be used with users being allocated their own private space.
- Users can share data.
- Backup procedures (see page 53) can be carried out centrally.

There are a number of ways that computers can be networked together and, while you do not need to know a great deal about the technical side of this, it is useful to be aware of the basics of how your system is set up.

Just as the computer needs software to enable the various parts to communicate – the operating system – it is necessary to have software for the network to run. This software is known as the network software.

CHECK IT YOURSELF

Is the computer you usually work on part of a network? What network software is used to run the system? What version number are you using at the moment? If the computer is part of a network, enter this information in section 1 of the software specification checklist on page 40.

Applications software

The software that is used to carry out the different tasks that you do is called applications software. Some of this may be general-purpose packages, which are also known as 'generic' software. These are packages which are very general in the way they are used; it is for the user to set them up for a range of different uses. This term is usually used to refer to word processing, spreadsheet, database, drawing and desk top publishing packages (see Figure 6).

CHECK IT YOURSELF

What 'generic' software is available on the system you usually use? For each package find out the name of the manufacturer, the name of the package and the version number. Enter these details in section 2 of the software specification checklist on page 40.

In addition to using these generic packages, there may be a number of very specific applications that are carried out on the computer which need software that has been written to carry out these particular jobs. These pieces of software may have been specially written for an organisation or may have

Software	What it does
Word processing 	Word processing software enables the creation, saving, editing and printing of documents.

Modern word processing facilities include not only sophisticated text manipulation and presentation functions but the facility for integration of data from other packages and the inclusion of graphical images. |
| **Spreadsheet**  | A spreadsheet is like a very large piece of paper that is divided into columns and rows, known as cells. What you can see on the screen at any one time is just a small part of the complete spreadsheet available to you. Calculations, using formulae, can be entered into cells and when the value in a cell is changed, all the formulae in the spreadsheet are automatically recalculated to give new results. |
| **Database** 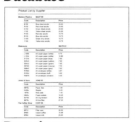 | A database gives you the capability to create an organised, structured collection of related data that can then be reorganised (sorted), selected and printed.

Queries can be made on the data to select the information before presenting it in a structured report. |
| **Drawing**  | Drawing software enables you to create pictures and other images, often with facilities to use a wide range of colours and effects. There are packages available for different types of drawing, e.g. painting, line drawing and computer-aided design (CAD). |
| **Desktop publishing**  | Desktop publishing (DTP) software can be used to create documents for publishing by manipulating text and images. Many word processing packages include basic DTP features while 'top of the range' DTP will produce copy ready for final printing. |

Figure 6 *Applications software*

been purchased from a general supplier and customised for the particular organisation or user. Some examples of this sort of package are payroll, accounting or production control.

Working with the equipment

When using the equipment, it is extremely important that you follow the guidelines of the manufacturer and/or the suppliers. If the equipment is not set up according to instructions it may well not function correctly; it could also be unsafe! Make sure that you do not attempt to connect or disconnect anything for which you are not trained or which is outside your authority. If you have not done a task before, such as changing a printer cartridge, get technical support and advice and always read the instruction manual first.

Setting up most equipment means not only the hardware but includes some software. When you connect a new printer to a computer it is usually also necessary to install the printer drivers, that is, the software that controls the output. Different printers need different codes from the computer to achieve a particular feature. Again, make sure that have authority to do this, that you follow any instructions fully and that you seek technical support if you are not sure of exactly what to do or have any difficulties during the process.

When you have finished using the equipment, make sure that you close down in the correct way. Whenever possible, you should exit from the software completely before switching off the computer. Failure to do so may result in loss of data or could leave temporary files on the system – these normally clear down automatically when you follow the correct procedures. Make sure you know which of the hardware should be turned off and how. This may be critical to other users of the system, particularly if you are working on a network. Don't switch off the network printer unless all the other users have finished as well, and you are authorised to do so.

Working with floppy disks

Most floppy disks need to be prepared before you can use them. This process is called *formatting*. You can buy preformatted disks, but you will have to pay more for them. It is a quick and easy task to format your own disks; the format command is provided as part of the operating system.

What does formatting do?

- It sets up the disk to be used in your type of disk drive (the number of tracks and sectors).
- It creates the root directory (which holds the information needed to locate files on the disk – see Unit 204, page 47).
- It checks the writing surfaces of the disk and informs you of any damage.
- It lets you give the disk a label (name).
- It deletes all existing data and file details.

Removable disks of all kinds are delicate items and need to be handled carefully. They can easily be damaged by:

- excessive heat;
- magnetic fields;
- dust;
- spilled drinks;
- bending and crushing; and
- damp.

Disks contain valuable data and software, so you need to take good care of them. Some of this data may be confidential and will need to be stored securely. The disks that are supplied with software on them are often not copiable, and therefore need to be held in a secure and safe place. All disks should be

- clearly labelled and dated – write on the label before you put it on the disk or use a pen with a soft tip; and
- stored in a suitable box with a lock and kept in a safe place.

Working with printers

Different types of printer

It is important you make sure that the printer you use is able to meet the requirements of the task. The 'client' may clearly specify what is required, e.g. the document must be printed in colour. But on many occasions it may be up to you to recommend the best solution. You will need to take account of the following:

- Volume – how many pages need to be printed?
- Time – is the speed of production critical?
- Quality – is it an internal or external document?
- Stationery – do you need to use special stationery?
- Colour – is colour required or 'true' black?

The advantages and disadvantages of each type of printer are shown in Figure 7.

Figure 7 *Types of printer: advantages and disadvantages*

Printer	Advantages	Disadvantages
Laser 	• High-quality print of both text and graphics • Reasonably fast models available • Quiet in operation • High-volume models available • Capable of printing on to acetates, envelopes and other specialist paper • Loading of paper relatively simple • Some models capable of printing on A3 paper	• Usually only able to handle maximum of A4 standard-weight paper • Not suitable for multi-part stationery • Use of heat and toner potential health hazard • Relatively high running costs • Colour models expensive – must use correct paper
Ink jet 	• High-quality print of both text and graphics • Quiet in operation • Capable of printing on to acetates, envelopes and other specialist paper • Loading of paper relatively simple • Reasonably inexpensive to buy • Good-quality colour models available and not expensive • Some models capable of printing on A3 paper	• Not suitable for multi-part stationery • Relatively slow unless in 'draft' mode • Relatively high running costs • Some paper will absorb too much ink, reducing the quality of print • Some colour models do not print 'true' black

Printer	Advantages	Disadvantages
Dot matrix	• Relatively cheap to buy and run • Some very high-speed printers available for high-volume printing • Capable of printing on multi-part stationery, e.g. sets of invoices • Wide-carriage models available for printing on wide paper	• Noisy – inevitable with an impact printer • Only near letter quality (NLQ) available – suitable only for internal reports and multi-part forms • Capable of only medium-quality graphics • Most models only work with continuous stationery • Correct loading of paper can be quite difficult

Managing the printer

Working effectively with printers can be quite a time-consuming activity. Unlike most other parts of the computer system, they are almost always produced by a different manufacturer and therefore have to be set up to meet your particular system's configuration. The applications software that you use will usually be supplied with a number of printer drivers – that is, programs that send the correct sequence of codes to the printer to enable all the print features to work correctly. You should usually find that the right one for your printer is available, but this is not always the case; it will depend on the model of the printer and the version of the software. It is not unusual to be running under a compromise set up which works most of the time, but can sometimes cause unexpected results.

Because the printer is external to the main system, and therefore the link is potentially fragile, it is always a good idea to save your work *before* you send it to the printer.

You need to make sure that you know how to do the following:

• Locate the on/off switch – but remember this should not normally be used to stop a print run as it may cause a paper jam, cancel any software settings for the font or paper orientation, or clear all the print instructions from the print queue.

• Find out which port it is connected to – this will probably be called LPT1 or something similar.

• Check the computer-to-printer cable – it should not be in a tangle, have any kinks, cuts or any signs of damage through crushing. It should be securely connected at both the computer port and at the socket in the printer.

- Load the paper tray or feed for continuous stationery – paper for laser and ink-jet printers must be loaded the right way up (there should be an arrow on the paper's packaging to indicate this). Continuous paper should be properly clipped on to the sprockets.

- Clear a paper jam safely – make sure the printer is switched off first and that you do not let your hair or any scarves/ties, clothing or items of jewellery fall into the equipment. (*Note*: You need to know the correct procedures and have the authority to open up the printer. If you don't, ask the technician or your supervisor to show you what to do so that you can do it under supervision next time.)

- Change a toner or ink cartridge or printer ribbon safely – this may need to take place at the same time as general maintenance and cleaning. You need to know details about the printer to make sure that you are using the correct cartridge or ribbon – the wrong one could cause serious damage. (See note above about opening printers.)

- Connect to a different printer – if you are working on a network you will need to know the software commands. Sometimes a number of users will share a number of printers through the use of a cross-over or T-switch; you will need to take the other users into consideration.

- Load letter-headed paper – the correct way up and round, and don't forget to take it out when you have finished.

- Use special paper and acetates. You must make sure that the correct paper or acetates are being used – the wrong type of acetate can cause an awful mess inside a laser printer! Paper that is too thick or the wrong size can jam inside the printer.

- Use sheets of labels. As with special paper, use the correct ones for your printer and check how to load them.

- Print on envelopes – most laser and ink-jet printers are capable of printing on to envelopes, and there is usually a special way to load them.

- Install a new printer driver – you will need to find out if you have authority to access the disk area where these are stored. Make sure that you inform other users of the changes you have made and how to use them. Sometimes a different printer driver could change the layout of a document by altering the page breaks or margin settings, and may also alter the fonts and special effects on a document.

Management of the area around the printer is also extremely important. Waste paper lying around the desk and floor is a potential health and safety hazard. Printers, or rather their users, always seem to generate far more sheets of paper than are wanted! There are many, mostly avoidable, reasons for this including the ones shown in Figure 8.

Wasted paper	Why?
Printing multiple copies in error	Check the printer – has someone forgotten to set it back to single copies?
Producing a blank sheet after each printout	The software installation may be wrong – speak to the technical support person
Unwanted printouts	Did you really need three or four copies?
Incorrect printouts	Did you proof-read, spellcheck, etc. before printing?

Figure 8 *The reasons for wasted paper*

CHECK IT YOURSELF

Who is responsible for the use of the printer, and what is done with the waste paper? Do you recycle your computer paper? Many organisations collect and process paper from computer printers. If your organisation simply throws away this paper, find out about services available locally and write a memo to make recommendations to your supervisor or manager.

As one of the organisation's 'computer experts' you need to make sure that you know where plain and letter-headed paper and labels are kept and how to use them. It is quite likely that others in the organisation will come to you for assistance in loading different types of paper, unjamming the printer, etc., and generally dealing with minor printer problems (see fault reporting page 44).

Using the fax

Fax machines are relatively simple to operate and most work in a very similar way, but you do need to familiarise yourself with all the basic operations. Fax machines can usually be set either to a fax or telephone setting – make sure you know how to do this.

Before sending a message, make sure that:

- the machine is switched on;
- the document feeder is correctly adjusted; and
- the machine is ready to transmit – it should be switched to fax.

So that the fax is always ready to receive messages, make sure that:

- the machine is switched on;
- the machine is switched to the fax setting;
- there is sufficient paper in the machine; and
- the ink cartridge is replaced when low.

Ensure that the area around the fax machine is kept tidy and free from waste paper. Does your fax machine just feed the printed faxes directly on to the floor? Suggest to your supervisor or manager the use of a basket or similar for them to feed into – this will keep the area tidy and also reduce the chance of a fax getting lost.

Computer specification checklist

Section 1: the computer	
Make	
Model	
Processor	
Processor speed	
RAM	
Hard disk	
No. of floppy disk drives	
Keyboard type	Extended (102) ☐ Standard ☐
Mouse	Yes/No No. of buttons:
VDU	Colour ☐ Monochrome ☐ VGA/SVGA?
Section 2: the printer	
Type	
Make	
Model	
Speed	
Quality	Colour ☐ Black on white only ☐
Section 3: other devices	
Storage devices:	
CD-ROM	
Other	
Input devices:	
Light pen	
Scanner	
Graphics tablet	
Digitiser	
Other	
Output devices:	
Sound card	
Plotter	
Other	

Software specification checklist

Section 1: the operating system	
Name	
Version number	
Environment	
Version number	
Network software	
Version number	
Section 2: applications software	
Type of application	Word processing
Manufacturer	
Name	
Version number	
Type of application	Database
Manufacturer	
Name	
Version number	
Type of application	Spreadsheet
Manufacturer	
Name	
Version number	
Type of application	
Manufacturer	
Name	
Version number	
Type of application	
Manufacturer	
Name	
Version number	
Type of application	
Manufacturer	
Name	
Version number	

Software specification checklist (continued)

Section 3: application specific	
Specific application	
Manufacturer	
Name	
Version number	
Specific application	
Manufacturer	
Name	
Version number	
Specific application	
Manufacturer	
Name	
Version number	
Specific application	
Manufacturer	
Name	
Version number	
Specific application	
Manufacturer	
Name	
Version number	

Unit 204 Contribute to the Effectiveness of the Information Technology Working Environment

This unit contains four elements:

204.1 Assist the maintenance of equipment and resources
204.2 Maintain your own file structures
204.3 Suggest areas for improvement
204.4 Assist the effective flow of work.

You need to demonstrate that you can use and maintain equipment and resources effectively. You will also need to show that you can organise and prioritise your work and that you can identify ways to improve the use of the technology.

To meet the requirements of this unit, you need to show that you can use resources effectively to minimise waste and can identify when resources need replenishing and to whom problems with resources should be reported. You should have a good basic understanding of where responsibility lies within the organisation for many aspects of the system's maintenance, both equipment and data. You should know about the procedures to carry out effective maintenance and to appreciate their importance to the organisation. You will also need to be aware of the scope and the limitations of your information technology working environment and the extent to which you can change it to improve the way you and others can work.

Information technology materials

There are two categories of materials that you will be working with – consumables and removable storage media.

Consumables

It is likely that you will need to produce output using a variety of different types of stationery. Most organisations use preprinted headed paper for their letters. If you are involved in the production of orders or invoices, there may be preprinted stationery. You may also need to produce address labels or even print directly on envelopes and, of course, you will need plain paper for much of your output. It is extremely important that you know how and when to use these materials (see Unit 202) but you also need to make sure you use them appropriately and that you have access to sufficient supplies to be able to work effectively.

It has been suggested frequently throughout the last thirty years that computers would bring about the 'paper-less office', but this has not yet happened. What has happened in many instances, probably because information can be more readily produced, is a significant increase in paper use. With the ease of use and speed of modern printing facilities, in many organisations much paper is wasted through unnecessary or careless printing. Do you check your output 'on-screen' before you print it, both for accuracy and appropriate layout? Do you print only the copies you need? How many unnecessary printouts get put in the recycling bin or, worse still, the rubbish? When working with plain paper this is of concern because of unnecessary wastage and cost, but when using specialist stationery it becomes more critical. Supplies of preprinted materials, labels, etc. are usually used in smaller quantities and your waste could result in not having sufficient available for a particular job.

Whatever type of printer you are using, you will also need to replace the ink or toner cartridge from time to time. You may not have responsibility for these supplies but will need to ensure that your printer is working effectively and will need to know where you get replacement cartridges from (see also Unit 201, page 36).

CHECK IT YOURSELF

You need to know what consumables you use, where they are located, who is responsible for ensuring there are sufficient supplies and what is the minimum level necessary. For each different type of consumable you use, enter this information in section 1 of the materials checklist on page 62.

Removable storage media

You will also need to store data regularly on removable storage media, most likely floppy disks and possibly CDs (see Unit 201). Again, you need to make sure you know how and when to use these materials but you also need to make sure you use them appropriately and that you have access to sufficient supplies to be able to work effectively.

Maintaining equipment

Fault reporting

One of the most frequent complaints concerning our dependence on computers is that they are always going wrong. In fact, this is not true, as very often the 'faults' are not problems with the equipment but arise because the users do not fully understand how to operate it or what the messages mean.

As an 'expert user', you need to make sure that you are able to recognise a true fault. Much of this comes from experience, but quite a lot is obvious if you think it through. If you ask your technical support team what are the most common faults reported to them they will undoubtedly tell you about:

- the printer not being connected or switched on;
- the monitor's contrast and brightness being turned right down;
- the network connection being unplugged; or
- the mouse with its ball removed

. . . and so the list goes on.

The other kinds of 'fault' that often arise are brought about by lack of knowledge as to how the software works:

- The printer prints gibberish or one line at the top of each page because the wrong printer driver is being used.
- The user is out of memory because there are too many windows open at the same time.
- The pictures in a document are missing from the printout because there is not enough disk space to create the print image.

The resolution of many faults can be speeded up if clear and precise information is passed to technical support staff. When you report a fault always make sure that you:

- copy down any error message exactly as it appears on the screen;
- note down the exact sequence that gave rise to the fault;

- give the precise location of the equipment – the floor, room and which machine if there is more than one in the room;
- give clear details of the equipment, e.g. the make and model number of the printer;
- give the date and time the fault occurred;
- report it to the right person – you may have different support for printers or network problems, for example; and
- alert support staff to any urgent deadlines to be met – they might be able to offer you access to an alternative computer or printer.

CHECK IT YOURSELF

Do you have your own error log to record problems and their solutions? If not, create an error logsheet; make sure that it includes sections for you to log the problem, when it occurred, the circumstances and the solution.

Cleaning the equipment

All the computer equipment, and the complete workstation, needs to be kept clean and – particularly – free from dust. Some of the responsibility for this may well be with technical support staff, but basic cleaning can be carried out by the user.

You need to make sure any cleaning materials you use are safe for you to handle. Read any instructions on the product before you use it and take care not to inhale fumes from cleaning fluids. There will usually be details on the packaging of any particular precautions necessary, such as the use of gloves. You must also make sure that the product is appropriate for the equipment – you can do more harm than good if you use the wrong cleaning substances. Always check in the manual, or with technical support staff, to find out any specific 'do's and don'ts'. Keep up to date with any new products by reading office equipment and computer magazines. Finally, make sure that any cleaning you do is carried out with the equipment switched off!

You may be expected to take responsibility for the cleaning of the following:

- *Disk drives*. This is similar to cleaning a music or video cassette. Floppy disk cleaners are available for running inside the disk drive, to clean the read/write heads and prolong the life of the drives, thereby reducing the risk of damage to your disks.
- *Mouse*. This is very prone to dirt, particularly the rollers that run on the ball. These can be cleaned using a cottonbud moistened with water. Make sure you use a mouse mat to reduce the level of dirt and to improve the performance of the mouse.

- *Mouse mat.* This is only useful if it is kept very clean and free from dust; a quick wipe-over once a week with a damp cloth can make all the difference.
- *Keyboard.* A wipe-over with a damp cloth will remove most dirt from sticky fingers.
- *Screen.* Anti-static screen wipes offer a quick way of cleaning and can make a great difference to the quality of the display.
- *Cases.* A regular wipe-over with a damp cloth will keep them clean.
- *Desk top.* Keep your desk top tidy, free from clutter and clean it regularly to ensure that it is dust free.

Do you know how much damage the spilling of a fizzy drink or cup of tea can do to a keyboard? The acid in a fizzy drink can completely destroy the electrical contacts in the keyboard; the milk or sugar in your tea are particularly sticky when dry and will stop the keys from working properly. If something gets spilled on a keyboard you should:

- turn off the equipment immediately;
- place the keyboard upside down; and
- notify technical support so that they can clean and check it.

CHECK IT YOURSELF

Are there rules about food and drink being brought near computers in your work area? Write a memo to your supervisor alerting him or her to the consequences of an accident with a drink.

Remember, you can use the time when you are cleaning the equipment to carry out some basic routine checks on cables, etc., to make sure that they are in good working order.

Working with files

Almost everything that is created using a computer can be stored in a file – the software you buy, the data you input, the letters and memos you type, and even most of the operating system that you use to make the computer work. These files are stored in directories or folders on a storage device.

Whatever computer system you are using, there will be a set of rules, controlled by the operating system, about the names you give to files and how you organise the storage.

If you are using an industry-standard PC, you will probably be using a version of Microsoft Windows. If you are using a different operating system you will need to find out the rules that apply to your computer.

Filenames

Every file has to have a name. This name must be unique to the storage area, directory or folder. The name must usually consist of only letters and numbers – many of the other characters on a keyboard have a special meaning in a filename. Files created in a Windows 95, or later, environment have two parts. The first part is given by the user, can also include spaces and can have up to 255 characters. The end of the first part of the name is indicated by the use of the full stop (.). This can then be followed by a second part, sometimes called the extension or suffix. This consists of up to three characters and will often be given automatically to the file by the specific application software, e.g. word processing documents often have a suffix of doc. The complete filename is recorded in a directory, or folder, and is used to access the file. The directory contains details about the file, usually the date and time it was created or last updated, where it is located on the disk and what size (in bytes) it is.

Directories and subdirectories

When a disk is first used in a computer it has to be set up. This is known as formatting (see Unit 201, page 32). Part of the disk is set aside to hold the directory information necessary to locate the files on the disk. This is known as the root directory and is referenced by the drive letter, a colon (:) and the back slash (\). For example, the root directory of the first floppy disk drive is referenced by A:\ . As it is possible to have a large number of files on any one disk, it is extremely important to organise them into subdirectories (folders) so that you can find them easily.

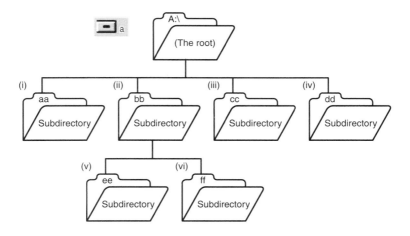

Figure 9 *Disk structure chart*

The system of subdirectories is hierarchical and is best understood through Figure 9. The paths are written as: (i) A:\aa, (ii) A:\bb, (iii) A:\cc, (iv) A:\dd, (v) A:\bb\ee and (vi) A:\bb\ff. Thus if all your documents relating to a sports and social club are stored on a floppy disk in subdirectory cc, you would find the minutes of the last committee meeting at A:\cc\mins298.

Case study: Crink, Totem & Partners

Chris works in a solicitor's office and carries out work on the computer for the three partners (Anna, Peter and David) in the firm. In the past two years 73 files have been created and they are all stored in the root directory. This often causes great difficulty in finding a particular file when it is needed.

Chris has decided that it would be a good idea to organise the files into subdirectories. The files include word processing documents (with doc suffix), produced for each of the partners, and also spreadsheets (with xls suffix) for Peter and Anna.

1 Draw a disk structure chart similar to the one in Figure 9 to show how you might organise Chris's disk into subdirectories and show this to your tutor.

2 Figure 10 lists the files and the names of the owners. Make a list for each subdirectory of the files that you would put into it.

Filename	Owner	Filename	Owner	Filename	Owner
letta1.doc	Anna	reporta1.doc	Anna	letta13.doc	Anna
costp3.xls	Peter	reportd2.doc	David	lettp21.doc	Peter
costa2.xls	Anna	lettd3.doc	David	lettd21.doc	David
letta5.doc	Anna	lettp2.doc	Peter	costa12.xls	Anna
lettp7.doc	Peter	lettp5.doc	Peter	costa20.xls	Anna
costa4.xls	Anna	lettd4.doc	David	costp21.xls	Peter
lettd10.doc	David	reportp4.doc	Peter	lettd25.doc	David
reporta3.doc	Anna	reporta6.doc	Anna	lettd26.doc	David
costp4.xls	Peter	costa3.xls	Anna	reporta20.doc	Anna
lettd8.doc	David	lettp6.doc	Peter	lettp22.doc	Peter
reportp1.doc	Peter	reportp5.doc	Peter	lettp23.doc	Peter

Filename	Owner	Filename	Owner	Filename	Owner
letta15.doc	Anna	costp13.xls	Peter	reportd22.doc	David
letta20.doc	Anna	reportd21.doc	David	lettd28.doc	David
lettd23.doc	David	letta21.doc	Anna	letta24.doc	Anna
reportd18.doc	David	letta23.doc	Anna	lettd29.doc	David
lettd24.doc	David	costa22.xls	Anna	costa23.xls	Anna
letta26.doc	Anna	lettd27.doc	David	reporta22.doc	Anna
reporta21.doc	Anna	reportp23.doc	Peter	lettp25.doc	Peter
costp22.xls	Peter	letta25.doc	Anna	letta27.doc	Anna
lettd30.doc	David	reportp24.doc	Peter	reportd24.doc	David
lettp26.doc	Peter	reportd25.doc	David	costa24.xls	Anna
lettd31.doc	David	costa25.xls	Anna	lettp27.doc	Peter
reporta23.doc	Anna	costp23.xls	Peter	lettp28.doc	Peter
lettd32.doc	David	reporta24.doc	Anna	lettd32.doc	David
costp24.xls	Peter				

Figure 10 *Files and their owners*

CHECK IT YOURSELF

Is the storage system you use at work or in college organised into subdirectories?

It would be a good idea to keep all the files you are going to use as evidence for your qualification separate from any of your work or exercise files. Find out from your tutor or supervisor how to set up directories on your system and create a subdirectory for each type of file (word processing, spreadsheet, database, picture). You may decide as your evidence collection progresses to amend this structure.

Now make a record of this using a disk structure chart similar to the one in Figure 9 (you may need to modify this to meet your particular system). Place this in your evidence portfolio.

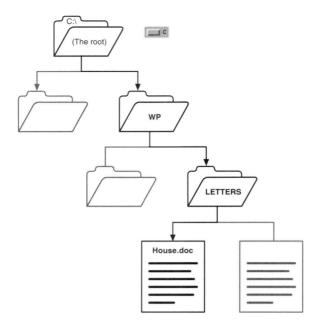

Figure 11 *Accessing a file through a path*

To access a file in a subdirectory you need to reference it through its *path*. The path is the way through the directory tree to where the file is. For example, if you are currently working in the root directory of disk Drive C and need to access a file called *house.doc* which is stored in a subdirectory called *LETTERS* which is itself in a subdirectory called *WP*, the path is *C:\WP\LETTERS\House.doc* (see Figure 11).

Case study: Crink, Totem & Partners

Write out the path that you have set up for the following:

1 Files belonging to Peter:

- lettp7.doc
- reportp23.doc
- costp21.xls

2 Files belonging to Anna:

- reporta1.doc
- costa12.xls
- letta23.doc

Data storage standards

Remember, the files that are created and stored while at work belong to the organisation. This means that they need to be accessible to authorised people within the organisation. Would your supervisor or a colleague be able to find a document you had created so that he or she could print a copy or make some amendments when you are on holiday or off sick or should you leave the organisation?

Data storage standards need to contain:

* filenaming conventions;
* filing systems; and
* recording systems.

Filenaming conventions

There need to be guidelines or rules as to what names are given to files. When working with most operating systems this can be quite difficult. As you should have found out, there are many rules and limitations about what names you can give to your files. You may also have found out how difficult it can be to find the file you want several weeks or months after you have created it.

CHECK IT YOURSELF

Are there guidelines or rules set down for what names you give to your files at work? Find out what they are. Who is responsible for setting these rules? Are they written down? Do they apply across the whole organisation or are they limited to a department or section? Are they reviewed? Enter this information in section 1 of the organisation standards checklist given on page 63.

If not, how do you decide on the names for your files?

Filing systems

There need to be guidelines or rules about where the files are stored. You know it can be almost impossible to find your files unless they are organised into subdirectories or folders but, like any filing system, it is important that others can find their way around as well as you.

Are there guidelines or rules for the organisation of your computer-based filing systems where you work? Find out what they are. Who is responsible for setting these rules? Are they written down? Do they apply across the whole organisation or are they limited to a department or section? Are they reviewed? Enter this information in section 2 of the organisation standards checklist on page 63.

Recording systems

Not only must your organisation's filenaming conventions and filing systems be adhered to but also the details of the files and the structure of your filing system need to be recorded. All systems require some sort of documentation. Just because data is held and organised on a computer does not mean that documentation is no longer necessary – in fact, in many respects it becomes more critical as most of your main filing system and data are electronically stored. It is often not as easy to scan quickly through a computer system to find the file you need as with one on paper.

Figure 12 *Disk directory printout*

Let us say that you create, on average, between 10 and 20 new files a day. After working for the organisation for six months you could have created more than 2000 files! If you, or anyone else, wanted to find a document you created on your first day, where would you start?

Many of these documents may have been amended or updated and sometimes you could have kept different versions for reference purposes. How will you know which version to use? To avoid wasting a considerable amount of time searching through your filing system it is important to maintain an easy-to-use recording system.

Large volumes of data and a considerable number of different files can be contained both online (stored on disks that are permanently connected to the computer) and offline (stored on disks that need to be loaded). There need to be records so that they can be easily located. What if the owner is not in the office? What happens when someone leaves the organisation? External bodies such as auditors also need to be able to find them, and so on.

For some of these records you can use the computer to produce the information. Printouts can give directory details for all disks (see Figure 12). A procedure is needed to specify how often these records are updated and where they are stored.

CHECK IT YOURSELF

Are there guidelines or rules at work for a recording system for your computer-based filing systems? Find out what they are. Who is responsible for setting these rules? Are they written down? Do they apply across the whole organisation or are they limited to a department or section? Are they reviewed? Enter this information in section 3 of the organisation standards checklist on page 63.

Housekeeping

As with any filing system, it is necessary for your computer files to be maintained regularly. It is very easy for large numbers of unnecessary files to be stored on your disks and to occupy considerable amounts of disk storage. The process of looking after your disk storage systems is known as housekeeping.

The main functions you will need to be familiar with in order to do this are those for *creating directories, copying, deleting, archiving* and making *backups*.

Backup procedures

In every computer environment, at work or at home, it is important that you keep backup copies of both the software on the system and of your work. Backup copies are kept for security reasons. The data that is stored on the main computer system will usually be 'live' data, that is, it is currently in use. It will include things like budgets that are being amended and/or monitored, ongoing correspondence which will still need to be referred to, minutes of meetings, etc.; in other words, the day-to-day work of the office. If these were 'lost' it would undoubtedly create extra work and could cause considerable disruption to the smooth running of the department or section of the organisation.

There are many reasons why you might lose your data:

- Floppy disks are very delicate and can be damaged quite easily.
- If the power goes off whilst the read heads are in contact with the hard disk you can experience what is known as a 'disk crash' and the whole disk may be completely destroyed.
- There are many viruses which can be brought into your computer that can destroy or corrupt your data.
- It is very easy to delete files by accident, but it can be very difficult to get them back.
- Unauthorised users may access files and accidentally or maliciously tamper with the data.

The *copy* command lets you make an exact copy of one or more files. However, this is limited in its use, particularly when the files to be copied are larger than the space available on a removable storage disk as it does not let you split a file between two or more disks. However, there are a pair of commands specifically designed to assist you with this procedure; one to make the backup copies and the other to restore the data should the original files become damaged or lost.

The *backup* command makes a copy of the files on to a numbered set of disks, prompting for the next disk as required. It does not, however, create readable or directly usable copies of the files. The usual way a backup command works is to create on each disk two files, one containing the data from the files and the second, often called a control file, identifying the names, sizes and creation dates of the files and also details of the sequence of the disk in the backup procedure.

The second command in the pair enables you to *restore* some or all of the data from these disks. It uses the information in the control file to find the data and to prompt you through the process as it restores the data from each disk.

These commands will usually allow you to carry out the backup procedure in a number of different ways. You can backup or restore:

- all the files in the directory;
- all the files in the directory and any subdirectories of that directory;
- only those files that have been updated or created on or after a specified date/time; and

- only those files updated or created since the last backup.

During the process you can:

- overwrite all previous files; or
- add files to those already on a backup disk.

In many organisations, particularly when working in a network environment, some of these procedures will be carried out centrally.

Archiving data

Archived files are not held for the same purpose as backups. Backup copies are held as security copies in case something happens to the originals. Archive copies are kept of files that are no longer needed in the main working environment but where a copy needs to be stored for reference or possible use in the future. It is quite common to keep electronic copies of old correspondence 'offline' – many accounting records need to be kept for seven years.

As these files are not going to be used regularly it does not make sense for them to be in the active working environment. They would need to be maintained and backed up if they were kept there and would occupy expensive, online storage space.

If you have carried out activities that you need for your 'evidence' but which are no longer needed for your work, it is best to archive them so that you still have them in electronic form without occupying valuable online storage space.

There are a number of different systems for storing archive copies of files. Essentially, these involve making copies which are held on some form of removable storage system, e.g. floppy disks, tape cartridge, microfiche or even CD-R.

Chris has now learned how to carry out housekeeping and wishes to 'tidy up' the hard disk. All the files that have a number of less than 20 in them are from previous years' work and do not need to be kept online. As 'hard copies' of all letters are in the paper files, it is not necessary to keep the out-of-date electronic files at all. However, the reports and spreadsheets need to be kept for at least five years.

Make lists of:

1 all the files to be deleted; and

2 the files to be archived on to floppy disk(s).

Discuss your decisions with your tutor.

CHECK IT YOURSELF

What procedures do you or your organisation carry out for archiving of data? Write a brief description of these procedures and place it in your evidence portfolio.

Documentation

Backup and archiving procedures must have permanent records to enable them to function correctly. Backup details need to be logged and tapes or disks need to be labelled appropriately. You need to know when the latest backup was taken and what updates have taken place if you are going to be able to restore your records in the event of some form of disaster.

CHECK IT YOURSELF

Find out what the documentation procedures are in your working environment for online data, backup systems and archived data. Add this detail to the notes you have made about the main procedures.

Organisation procedures

A whole range of activities associated with computer-based work are tasks that need to be carried out regularly, always in the same way and in accordance with a set of guidelines. To ensure that all staff who might be responsible for these activities know exactly what needs to be done, many organisations will have set written procedures.

Figures 13 and 14 show examples of guidelines for storage in one organisation. We have already looked at a number of such activities in the sections on housekeeping and working with data. You may already have copies of the following procedures:

- backup and restore;
- archiving; and
- recording of online data.

Within an organisation, these procedures may all be written in a similar way. Just as it is easier to learn to use another software package if it uses similar menus and terms to one you already know, so it is helpful to present all the procedures in a similar way.

Looking after your evidence

You will need to check what the commands are for your operating system or environment. As this is a fundamental part of working with computers make sure you are really confident about using these commands.

Set aside a time at least once a week to carry out the housekeeping of the disks and files that contain the evidence for your qualification, or it will become such a large task that it won't get done. There are a number of tasks that should be done regularly:

- *Delete* all files that are no longer needed.
- *Move* all files into the right subdirectories – there always seem to be some in the wrong place, no matter how careful you are at the time of creating them!
- Carry out *backup* procedures.
- *Archive* files that are no longer needed in the main work area.
- *Record* all these activities.

Identifying areas for improvement

Customising setups

When software is installed it is usually put on to the system with the default setups as supplied by the manufacturer. However, this is often not the particular way in which you or your organisation wishes to use the package. The software will need to be set to get the best from your particular hardware in terms of use of memory, type of printing facilities and most frequently used aspects of the package. Most organisations will want to have a level of standardisation in terms of printed output to present a corporate image (see also page 101–103).

Many organisations will require that all their users have the same setup for ease of maintenance and upgrading, while some aspects of the computer

File storage guidelines

It is the responsibility of all computer users to ensure that their work is correctly saved and stored on the appropriate storage system. All access points (terminals) are provided with access to the company's network and also a local hard drive.

Local hard drive
The maintenance of data stored on the hard drive is entirely the responsibility of the users.

It is recommended that:

- each user stores work in a separate subdirectory/folder
- shared files are stored in a department/section subdirectory/folder
- a designated person has responsibility for operation of the backup procedures
- a departmental standard for filenames is operated
- individual users have responsibility for archiving long-term data
- individual users have responsibility for managing own data.

Department/section network areas
The maintenance of data stored in the network is primarily the responsibility of the **owner** department.

It is recommended that:

- a designated person within the department has overall responsibility for maintenance of the network area
- a departmental directory/folder structure is established and maintained
- a departmental standard for filenames is operated
- the department has responsibility for archiving long-term data – any data that has not been accessed for more than three months will be deleted from the system.

Central Computer Services will carry out routine backup procedures on a **weekly** basis. It is **strongly** recommended that the department carries out more frequent backup procedures.

Restore procedures
Requests for restoring data on the network must be made in writing to Computer Services. This must include details of the network area, directory path, filenames and date last modified.

Figure 13 *An organisation's file storage procedures*

Administration Department
File storage guidelines

It is extremely important to ensure that all data storage systems are maintained and that adequate records are kept within the department. The data that is held on the company-wide network is **more** secure than that held on the local hard disk. All work of a confidential nature should therefore be stored on the network.

Department network areas
Each member of staff has a secure, passworded area on the network and will be required to change the password at least every 30 days. Passwords should **never** be disclosed to anyone else. All members of the department also have access to a department area for storing shared data. The password for this area is changed by the office manager every 25 days and notified to all staff in the department.

- The **department area:** within this there are directories for each of the members of staff (staff member's name). If you need to subdivide your data further, you **must** notify the office manager of the name and purpose of the folder.
- For own **separate area:** within this the individual is responsible for setting up an appropriate structure.

Local hard disks
As the three computers in this section are used by all staff within the department, data needs to be organised to ensure that access to required files is straightforward and that other users are not likely to damage files accidentally.

- For **shared data:** the directory **Admin** has been set up. Within this there are directories for each of the members of staff (staff member's name). If you need to subdivide your data further, you **must** notify the office manager of the name and purpose of the folder.
- For own **separate data:** each member of staff has a directory based on his or her name. Within this, the individual is responsible for setting up an appropriate structure.

Filenames
All filenames should include the initials of the owner and clearly indicate the content of the document. All files kept on either the network or the local hard disk should be entered on to the disk log sheet. This must include the filename, the author, the date created and a clear description of content.

Archiving
All work that is no longer required online (either on the network or the local hard drive) should be deleted or archived on to floppy disk. All data on archive disks should be recorded on archive log sheets. Data in the network area that has not been accessed for more than three months will be deleted by Computer Services – make sure that it has been archived if it is needed.

Departmental backups
Computer Services will back up network data on a weekly basis.
The office manager will carry out network backups of modified files **only** for the **department** area on a daily basis (at 5.15 pm). It is the responsibility of individual owners to take more frequent backups of their own areas. The office manager will ensure that a full backup is taken of all the local drives weekly. It is the responsibility of individual owners to take more frequent backups of their own areas. All records of departmental backups will be kept in the department general office.

Restore procedures
Requests for restoring data on the network must be made in writing to Computer Services. This must include details of the network area, directory path, filenames and date last modified. Data can only be restored to the local hard disk with the authorisation of the office manager.

Figure 14 *A department's file storage procedures*

desktop may be customised to suit the individual user. For most people there is an optimum colour scheme which causes least stress and may even improve productivity.

Automation of functions

For most computer users, many of their tasks are done on a regular basis. Whether it is extracting sets of information from a database or typing a memo, many aspects of the activity are the same. It therefore makes sense to find ways of reducing the repetition and of getting the computer to assist you in your work. It is often relatively simple to automate or semi-automate these tasks using some of the more advanced features of the software package.

Most business software in use today have a feature called a *macro*. Macros are small routines which can be predefined to carry out a sequence of instructions or events within the software. Once they have been defined they can be run, or executed, whenever required. These macros may be very small, simple routines or may be quite complex and interactive with the user – for example, to complete a standard form.

1 description of the task;

2 details of how it could be improved, including:

- speed of production,
- improved accuracy of the data,
- improved quality of presentation, and
- reduction in technical expertise required;

3 details of the resources necessary to make this change (if any);

4 implications for the users (changes in way they work);

5 implications for other users (e.g. change in the version of the software); and

6 timescale to implement (include retraining programme if appropriate).

Identifying and prioritising tasks

It is likely that most of the tasks you are expected to do are generated by other people. Much of the work will be for routine activities that you will be required to carry out regularly. For example, you may need to enter the regional sales figures into a spreadsheet every week and then send a printout to each of the regional managers. It would be your responsibility to make sure that the changes were *accurate*, that the job is done *on time* and the task is *completed* by either printing it out and circulating the hard copy, or by sending an electronic version to those who need this information.

There are also likely to be times when your supervisor gives you a non-routine job to do. For example, you may be asked to produce a revised form for recording staff holiday details.

When there are a number of tasks to be done, you need to organise your workload and decide your priorities. Sometimes it is not easy to decide which job should be done first. For jobs that you carry out regularly it should be reasonably straightforward, as you know what is involved, how long it is likely to take and you will usually have a good idea as to how critical the completion time is. However, it is more difficult to assess non-routine tasks as they are, by their very nature, unpredictable. You may need to seek guidance from your supervisor when deciding priorities involving something that you do not do regularly and it may be even more important to alert the 'customer' if there are likely to be any difficulties with meeting deadlines.

Materials checklist

Section 1: consumables	
Plain stationery	Yes ☐ No ☐
where stored	
person responsible	
minimum level	
Letterheaded stationery	Yes ☐ No ☐
where stored	
person responsible	
minimum level	
Labels	Yes ☐ No ☐
where stored	
person responsible	
minimum level	
Envelopes	Yes ☐ No ☐
where stored	
person responsible	
minimum level	
Other stationery	Type
where stored	
person responsible	
minimum level	
Section 2: removable storage media	
Floppy disks	Yes ☐ No ☐
where stored	
person responsible	
minimum level	
Writable CDs	Yes ☐ No ☐
where stored	
person responsible	
minimum level	
Other removable storage media	Type
where stored	
person responsible	
minimum level	

Organisation standards checklist

Section 1: filenames	
Is there a set of guidelines?	Yes ☐ No ☐
Who is responsible for setting them?	
Are they written down?	Yes ☐ No ☐
Are they for the whole organisation or the department?	Organisation ☐ Department ☐
Is there a system for review?	Yes ☐ No ☐
Section 2: filing systems	
Is there a set of guidelines?	Yes ☐ No ☐
Who is responsible for setting them?	
Are they written down?	Yes ☐ No ☐
Are they for the whole organisation or the department?	Organisation ☐ Department ☐
Is there a system for review?	Yes ☐ No ☐
Section 3: recording systems	
Is there a set of guidelines?	Yes ☐ No ☐
Who is responsible for setting them?	
Are they written down?	Yes ☐ No ☐
Are they for the whole organisation or the department?	Organisation ☐ Department ☐
Is there a system for review?	Yes ☐ No ☐

Improvements checklist

Section 1: customising	
Has the software been customised?	Yes ☐ No ☐
Do you have the authority to make any changes?	Yes ☐ No ☐
If not, who does?	
Is there a procedure to propose changes?	Yes ☐ No ☐
What changes would you propose?	

1

2

Section 2: automation	
Are there any automated functions?	Yes ☐ No ☐
Do you have the authority to define your own?	Yes ☐ No ☐
If not, who does?	
Is there a procedure to propose and record them?	Yes ☐ No ☐

What automation would you propose?

Unit 206 Ensure Your Own Actions Reduce Risks to Health and Safety

This unit contains two elements:

206.1 Identify the hazards and evaluate the risks in your workplace

206.2 Reduce the risks to health and safety in your workplace.

You need to demonstrate that your actions do not create health and safety risks and that you do not ignore significant risks in your workplace. You will also need to demonstrate that you take appropriate and sensible actions to put things right.

To meet the requirements of this unit, you should have a good basic understanding of where responsibility lies for health and safety within your organisation. You should know about the legislation that relates to the workplace and particularly to working in an information technology environment. You will also need to be able to identify risks arising from hazards and know what you can deal with safely and what should be reported to a 'responsible person'.

Most people spend a considerable amount of time in their working environment. You should be aware of what potential hazards there are and the legislation that exists concerning health and safety. As the working environment changes and there is a greater use of new technology you should understand the particular health and safety factors involved.

There are two main aspects to consider:

- general health and safety; and
- working in an information technology environment.

General health and safety

The main piece of legislation that relates to general health and safety is the Health and Safety at Work Act 1974. This legislation makes both the employer and the employee responsible for ensuring that the workplace is a safe and suitable place to work.

Employers must:

- ensure that the workplace is safe and without risks to their employees' health;
- ensure that the workplace is clean and control the levels of dust, fumes and noise;
- ensure that both plant and machinery are safe to work with and that safe work practices are set and followed;
- provide their employees with all necessary information, instruction, training and supervision for health and safety;
- put in place and implement a health and safety policy;
- provide any protective clothing and equipment that is specifically required by health and safety legislation;
- report injuries, diseases and dangerous incidents to the appropriate enforcing authority;
- provide adequate first aid facilities and training;
- take adequate precautions to prevent fire and provide appropriate means of fire fighting;
- provide adequate means of escape;
- maintain a workroom temperature of at least 16°C after the first hour of work where employees do most of their work sitting down;
- provide, maintain and keep clean washing and toilet facilities;
- ensure that employees do not have to lift, carry or move any load so heavy that it is likely to injure them; and
- ensure that objects and substances are stored and used safely.

As an employee, you are required to be responsible for the health and safety of yourself and others and must cooperate with your employer and:

- follow the organisation's routine health and safety procedures and practices;
- take appropriate action if a hazardous or potentially hazardous situation arises; and
- ensure that your own work area is tidy and free from hazards.

Hazards in the working environment

Many aspects of the working environment present a hazard or potential hazard. Hazards are those aspects of the environment, the equipment and working practices which are unsafe. A potential hazard is often something less obvious.

When does a potential hazard become a hazard? This could result from:

- carelessness or lack of attention;
- lack of foresight;
- rushing tasks or taking short-cuts;
- a coincidence of circumstances; or
- a change in circumstances.

Almost all hazards are preventable if thought about beforehand.

Most workplaces have potential hazards which can result in accidents, including the following:

- A shiny floor turns into a skating rink when a cup of coffee is spilt on it.
- An open window is caught by a sudden strong gust of wind, slams shut and shatters.
- A fizzy drink beside the computer is knocked over which damages the keyboard and also causes an electrical hazard.
- A filing cabinet drawer next to a desk is left open where someone could walk into it.
- A computer is moved to another part of the room causing stress on the cables as they only just reach.
- Particles of toner are being continually released into the air from the laser printer in the main working area.
- Passageways are obstructed.
- Cables are frayed or damaged.
- Plugs are unearthed.

What should you do about a hazard? If it is within your control, deal with it. For example,

- make sure that when boxes of stationery are delivered they are put away safely;
- move the waste bin from the passage way before someone trips over it; and
- explain the dangers of using a swivel chair to stand on.

If it isn't within your control, report it to someone who can deal with it.

CHECK IT YOURSELF

You should be able to recognise the commonly used safety symbols. In Figure 15 there are a number of standard health and safety signs and symbols. Complete the details of what they stand for. Locate examples of these in your workplace and note this down on the chart.

Sign	Indicates
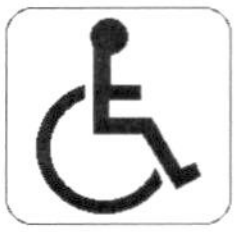	
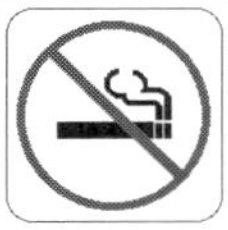	
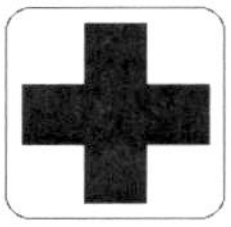	
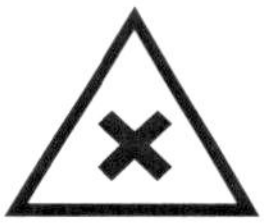	
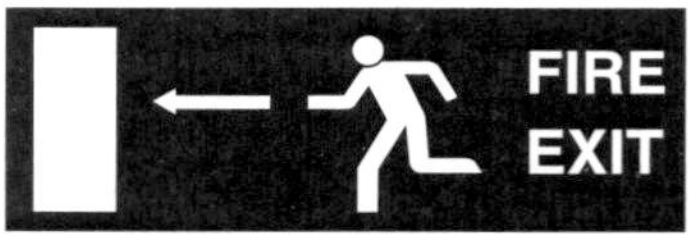	
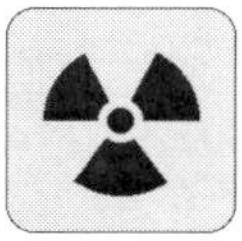	
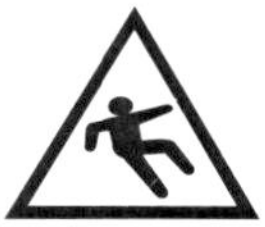	
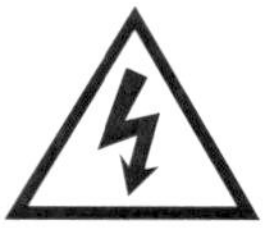	

Figure 15 *Identify these health and safety signs and symbols*

Figure 16 shows a typical modern office. However, it is not a wholly safe working environment. Draw up two lists, one containing existing hazards and the other to include aspects that have the potential to be unsafe. Identify which of these would be within your authority to deal with and what you would do in each case. What procedures would you follow for those which were outside your authority? Include this information and a copy of the picture in your evidence folder.

Figure 16 *Identify the hazards in this working environment*

Emergencies

Accidents

Employers are required to take all reasonable steps to make sure that the workplace is a safe environment. Any accidents that do occur must be reported and recorded. This record has to be kept for 30 years. The circumstances of the accident must be investigated and, if it is serious, may have to be reported to the Health and Safety Executive (HSE).

What is the procedure in your working environment for reporting and recording accidents? What information is recorded and who is responsible for maintaining these records? Enter this information in section 1 of the health and safety checklist given on page 79.

First aid

Under the Health and Safety (First Aid) Regulations organisations are required to provide first aid facilities including qualified first aiders, first aid boxes and sometimes a first aid room. The level of provision is determined on the basis of the size of the organisation and how hazardous the environment is deemed to be. An office is potentially far less hazardous than a building site, for example. First aid boxes are not allowed to contain drugs nor can first aiders give out any medication - they could leave themselves open to legal action if someone had an adverse reaction to a drug he or she had been given.

What first aid facilities are provided in your workplace? The names and contact numbers of all first aiders should be prominently displayed. Can you locate this information? What is kept in the first aid box nearest to your work area? Enter all of this information in section 2 of the health and safety checklist on page 79.

Illness

If you are ill at home, you will normally be required to notify your supervisor, line manager or tutor that you are unable to come to work. You would then possibly arrange to see your GP. However, there may be times when you or a colleague becomes unwell while at work. In some instances, it may be necessary for a person who is unwell to go home. The person's supervisor should be notified, and assistance may be needed to get home.

In situations where an emergency arises, and you do not know the correct thing to do, make sure that you call a first aider immediately and don't try to deal with something outside your own scope. This can often make things much worse.

Many organisations will welcome requests by staff to become first aiders and will provide the necessary training. The expertise and knowledge that you get on a first aid course are extremely valuable to you not just at work, so consider finding out about this.

Fire

Employers can take a number of precautions against fire. For example, they can:

- install fire doors;
- install fire extinguishers;
- install smoke detectors and sprinkler systems;
- restrict or ban smoking; and
- arrange regular fire inspections by the fire brigade.

CHECK IT YOURSELF

If there were a fire, would you know what to do? Do you know the fire procedures in your workplace? If not, find out. Are details posted around the building? Who is responsible for ensuring that there are adequate notices and information for all occupants of the building? Write a brief report outlining all this and place it in your evidence folder.

For the purposes of fire-fighting, fires are grouped into different types (see Figure 17). A range of different fire extinguishers is available to deal with each of those (see Figure 18).

Class of fire	*Substance burning*
A	Paper, wood, fabric
B	Liquids, fat, paint, spirits, oil
C	Gases such as oxygen
D	Metals such as magnesium
Electrical	

Figure 17 *Types of fire*

Colour	Contents	Class of fire
Red	Water	A
Green	Halon, BCF	A, B, C, electrical
Cream	Foam	A, B, C
Chrome	Gas	A, B, C, electrical
Black	CO_2	B, C, electrical
Blue	Powder	D

Figure 18 *Types of fire extinguisher*

CHECK IT YOURSELF

In the area where you carry out most of your computer work, is there a fire extinguisher? What type is it? Is it appropriate for your area? Add this detail to your report on fire procedures.

Fire extinguishers should be checked regularly to ensure they are ready for use when needed. This information should be displayed on each extinguisher.

CHECK IT YOURSELF

When was the fire extinguisher in your work area last checked? Find out who is responsible for this task. Has it ever been used? Add this information to your report. When the report is complete, give a copy to your supervisor, making sure it identifies any potential hazards or breaches of the legislation.

Evacuation

There are a number of circumstances, in addition to fire, when it may be necessary to evacuate the building. These include:

- bomb threats;
- severe flooding; and
- gas leaks.

The organisation where you work should have regular fire/evacuation drills and the alarms should be tested frequently to ensure they all work.

Working in an information technology environment

There are still many uncertainties about aspects of a modern, technology-based working environment. Even now, not a great deal of information is available about the long-term effects of working in this kind of environment. Many people are understandably anxious about the possible effects, and in the past few years there has been a tightening up of the regulations and legal obligations of employers. The main legislation that relates to employers' obligations is primarily concerned with the use of display screen equipment (VDUs).

Health and Safety (Display Screen Equipment) Regulations 1992

The display screen equipment directives and regulations contain very specific requirements of the employer in relation to employees working with VDUs. You should be aware that these regulations apply *only* to employees. However, they are based upon good, safe working practice and ideally should exist in *all* computer areas, at home, work or college.

Regulation 1: the user

The regulations define a user as an employee required to work at:

- a workstation on the employer's premises;
- a workstation at home; or
- a workstation on another employer's premises.

The following factors are helpful in deciding if an employee is a user covered by regulations:

- The person relies on the use of display screen equipment to do the job.
- The person has no choice as to whether to use the equipment.
- Specific skills or training in the use of the equipment are necessary to do the job.
- The job can be carried out only through the use of the equipment for continuous spells of an hour or more at a time on a regular basis, probably daily.

- The job requires the fast transfer of information between the user and screen.
- The job demands high levels of attention and concentration by the user.

(*Note*: the definition of equipment excludes calculators, cash registers and typewriters with a small display screen.)

CHECK IT YOURSELF

Do you qualify as a *user*? Would you qualify, but for the fact that you are a student or trainee rather than an employee?

Regulation 2: risk analysis

This requires that the employer carries out a workstation assessment. This assessment must be a suitable and sufficient analysis to assess the health and safety risks users may be exposed to as a result of using the equipment. It must include all workstations used by employees regardless of who actually provided them.

The assessment should identify the risks in the *work space*:

- Is the workstation designed and positioned so that the user is able to change position?
- Is the room lighting satisfactory and does it provide adequate contrast?
- Are there reflections and glare?
- What levels of noise are emitted by the equipment?
- What levels of heat are generated by the equipment?
- Are there more than negligible levels of radiation, other than those in the visible part of the electromagnetic spectrum?
- Are adequate humidity levels established and maintained?

It should also identify risks involved in using *interfaces*:

- Is the software suitable for the task?
- Is the software easy to use and, where appropriate, can it be adapted to the level of knowledge or experience of the operator?
- Does the software provide feedback to the operator on performance of those systems?
- Does the software display information in a format and at a pace that can be adapted to meet the needs of the operator?

The assessment will often identify a number of areas for concern, and these will need further evaluation and corrective action to reduce the risks.

The codes of practice identify three general categories of risk to health:

Bad posture

- Most of these risks may be overcome by simple adjustments to ways of working.
- They will often highlight the need for training.

Damage to eyesight

- These risks may need simple remedies only such as repositioning of the equipment or the use of blinds.
- Glare and reflections can be prevented by coordinating workplace and workstation artificial light.

Fatigue and stress

- These risks may be reduced by considering the design of workstations.
- Remedies will often involve reviewing rest periods or the pace of work.

Regulation 3: new workstations

Since 1997 the employer has had to ensure that **all** workstations meet the requirements laid down in the schedules to the regulations.

Regulation 4: breaks

The employer is required to organise the activities of users so that their daily work using display screen equipment is regularly interrupted by breaks or changes of activity to reduce their continuous workload at that equipment.

The codes of practice recommend that:

- breaks should be taken *before* fatigue sets in and not to recuperate from it;
- frequent short breaks are preferable; e.g. five to ten minutes every hour; and
- breaks should be taken *away* from the display screen.

Jobs that involve a mixture of screen and non-screen work may well have sufficient breaks away from the screen to make scheduled breaks unnecessary.

Regulation 5: eyes and eyesight

If you are a regular, substantial user of display screen equipment or about to become one, you are entitled to ask for eye and eyesight tests. They must be carried out as soon as practicable by a competent person and usually before you become a user. Thereafter, regular check-ups may be requested.

Where it is found that you need special corrective appliances (usually special spectacles) the cost of these has to be borne by the employer. It does not cover persons who need normal eyesight correction, but only where a special type is required to deal specifically with a problem in using VDUs.

Regulation 6: provision of training

Where an employee is a user or is about to become a user, the employer must ensure that:

- the employee is provided with adequate health and safety training in the use of any workstation upon which he or she may be required to work; and
- whenever there is any substantial modification to the workstation the user must be provided with adequate health and safety training.

Regulation 7: provision of information

The employer must ensure that:

- all users are provided with adequate information about all aspects of health and safety relating to their workstation; and
- users are informed of measures taken by the employer in compliance with duties under regulation 2 (assessment) and regulation 3 (workstations) as relate to them and their work.

CHECK IT YOURSELF

Find out who is responsible in your working environment for ensuring that the organisation complies with health and safety regulations. If there are breaches of the regulations, to whom would you report them – your immediate supervisor, a health and safety representative, your tutor?

Good practice when working with VDUs

There are many examples of good practice which can reduce risks to your health. Many of these you can introduce yourself, while others will require the cooperation and support of your employer or colleagues.

Figure 19 shows correct posture when seated at your workstation and the positioning of the equipment in relation to you.

One of the most important aspects of your workstation is that it should be adjustable to fit you or whoever is working there. When you get into the driving seat of a car you adjust the seating position for comfort and safe access to the controls. You should do the same when you sit down at a workstation.

Always check the following.

The height of your chair
- You should have sufficient space below the desk top to be able to move your legs freely.

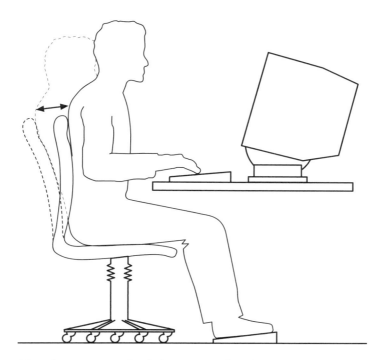

Figure 19 *Correct posture for sitting at a workstation*

- You may need a foot rest so that the back of your legs and knees do not have excess pressure on them.
- Your arms should be horizontal and your eyes should be on a level with the top of the VDU.

The support of your chair
- Your back should be supported but without undue pressure.

Mobility of your sitting position
- You should not sit in the same position for too long.
- You need to be able to move the position of your chair with ease in relation to the workstation and the different tasks you are likely to carry out.

The image on the screen
- Adjust the brightness and contrast so that they are comfortable for you – the image should be sharply focused and easy to read.
- Clean your screen regularly, as dirt and finger marks distort the image.
- Choose appropriate colour schemes where possible.

The layout of the workstation
- Move the keyboard, mouse mat, mouse and monitor to meet your work needs.

- Are you left or right handed? You can change your mouse installation to accommodate this.
- Make sure that you don't need to bend your hands up at the wrists when using the keyboard.
- Make sure you have sufficient space for papers, disk boxes, etc. If you frequently work from paper documents, a document holder may improve the comfort of your workstation. A cluttered workspace will make for reduced productivity as well as fatigue.

The lighting conditions in the room
- Bright lights should not reflect on the screen – you may need blinds to reduce sunlight at certain times of the day.
- The location of the workstation needs to take into account both natural and artificial lighting.
- Do you have sufficient light on the papers you are working from?

CHECK IT YOURSELF

How safe and suitable is your workstation? Complete the health and safety checklist 2 on page 80 to carry out an assessment. Speak to your supervisor about any problems you find and discuss what changes can be made.

RSI (repetitive strain injury)

This is a condition from which quite a number of people suffer. It is an extremely painful and sometimes quite debilitating injury. It is most likely to occur in people who are carrying out small, rapid, movements of the hands, fingers and wrists. It would appear to be something that can be brought about by incorrect posture at the keyboard or excessive use without rest. Typists on old typewriters were less likely to get it because the range of movement required to operate a manual keyboard was much greater. Using a mouse, particularly for long periods of time without a break, can also be a cause.

The best thing for you to do, particularly if you use a keyboard or mouse for long periods at a time, is to make sure that:

- you have set the keyboard so that it is most comfortable for you;
- you position your hands correctly over the keys; and
- you take suitable breaks.

Health and safety checklist 1

Section 1: accidents	
Is there a formal procedure for reporting accidents? If yes, place a copy in your evidence folder	Yes ☐ No ☐
What information is recorded in the accident record book?	Details of the injured person ☐
	Details of the injury ☐
	Details of the accident
	Date ☐
	Time ☐
	Place ☐
	What happened ☐
	Treatment received ☐
	Name of witness (if any) ☐
Details of responsible person	Name:
	Job title:
Section 2: first aid	
What is the name of your nearest first aider? How can you contact him or her?	
What is kept in your nearest first aid box?	Individually wrapped sterile bandages ☐
	Sterile eye pads ☐
	Triangular bandages ☐
	Safety pins ☐
	Eye bath ☐
	Sterile water for eye baths ☐
	Sterile wound dressings in different sizes ☐
	Other:
Section 3: evacuation	
Name of responsible person	
Date and time of last evacuation drill you took part in	

Health and safety checklist 2: workstation assessment

	Yes	No
Screen		
Is the screen large enough?		
Is the image stable and flicker-free?		
Can you adjust the image so that it is sharply focused?		
Can you adjust the colour scheme to suit your needs?		
Can you adjust the angle of the screen?		
Keyboard		
Is the keyboard of an appropriate size?		
Can you feel or hear the keys when pressed?		
Is there sufficient space to arrange it to suit your needs?		
Workstation		
Is your chair comfortable?		
Is the seat height and tilt adjustable?		
Is the height of the back-rest adjustable?		
Is the back-rest adjustable to fit your back?		
Does the chair swivel?		
Is the chair mobile?		
Have you been given information on adjusting your chair?		
Do you have sufficient leg room?		
Can you adjust the height of the desk top?		
Do you need a foot-rest?		
Is a foot-rest provided?		
Is a document holder available?		
Do you have sufficient work space?		
Working environment		
Is there excessive glare in the work area?		
Are there reflections on your screen from the window?		
Are blinds fitted in the room?		
Are the lights too bright?		
Do you need more directed lighting?		
Is the desk top too shiny?		

Unit 208 Improve Your Own Effectiveness in the Information Technology Working Environment

This unit contains two elements:

208.1 Develop your IT effectiveness within your job role
208.2 Develop effective working relationships with colleagues.

You need to demonstrate that you can identify your IT development requirements in order to carry out your job role. You will also need to show that you can develop effective working relationships with your colleagues and managers.

To meet the requirements of this unit, you should have a good basic understanding of your job role and the skills and knowledge required to do it effectively. You should know how to access training opportunities, including self-study. You should also understand the structure of your organisation or department and how to work with and support others. You will need to understand the different types and styles of personal communications and when each should be used.

When you have gained your qualification, you should be well on the way to being an 'expert user'. As you progress towards this award, you will become increasingly aware of the range of skills and knowledge that this implies. Your colleagues and employers will expect you to be able to advise and recommend better ways of using the existing facilities as well as improvements or enhancements that could be made to the software and hardware.

To be able to do this effectively you need to be confident in the skills that you have, aware of the limitations of your knowledge and, therefore, of when and where to seek support or assistance. You need to be adventurous in your use of computer systems and determined that your skills and knowledge stay current (up to date). In the world of technology, you can't stand still for too long!

The organisation

NVQs are about the workplace. It is therefore necessary that you know about how organisations may be structured and how these structures can affect different aspects of working relationships.

Organisational structure

Organisational structure defines the lines of authority and reporting. It defines where particular activities take place and how control is exercised. For most of us, the structure of the organisation we work for is often not apparent. We carry out the tasks we are required to do and often are not aware of the wider functioning of the whole.

However, when you are using data that is on a computer system, it is frequently data that is available across the whole organisation. The data that you input into the database or the form that you create is often going to be used by both the people that you work with on a day-to-day basis and others whom you do not know and quite often are not aware of. It is therefore essential for you to know at least a little about the way your organisation is structured.

Most organisations have a written document showing their structure. This is usually drawn as a chart. In a large organisation this may consist of a general organisation chart detailing the different departments or sections and how they work together and separate charts to show the staffing structure (line management) in each department. For smaller organisations there may be just one chart that shows both the departmental and staffing details.

Case study: Avits Ltd

Alan and Vayo Tomas jointly own a company which makes and sells 3D Wingdings. Alan heads the design team and looks after production while Vayo oversees sales, finance and general administration. The organisation chart of Avits Ltd is shown in Figure 20.

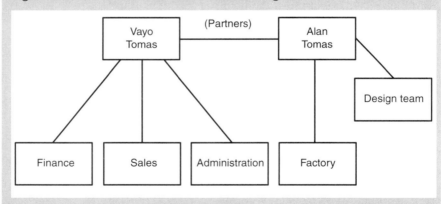

Figure 20 *Avits Ltd: organisation chart*

The structure of each department is shown in Figure 21.

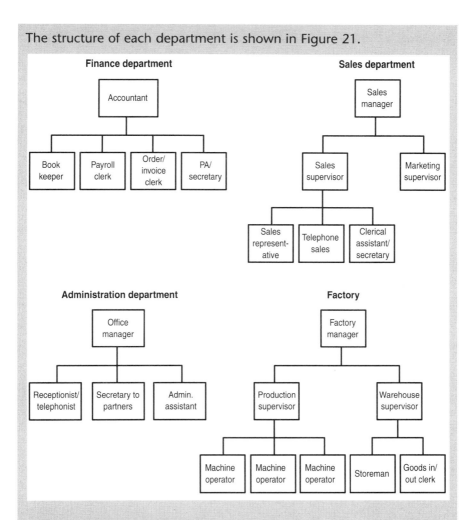

Figure 21 *Avits Ltd: departmental structure*

Using the information in Figures 20 and 21, identify the line manager of the following staff:

1 Goods in/out clerk at the factory.
2 Payroll clerk in the finance department.
3 Sales supervisor in the sales department.
4 Accountant.
5 Secretary to the partners.

Confirm your answers with your tutor.

What is the structure for the organisation where you work or are gaining your work experience? Ask your supervisor for a copy of the organisation chart if there is one. If you are in a small organisation which has not created one, find out what the structure is and draw one of your own. You may wish to check with your supervisor to make sure that you have understood the organisation correctly – he or she may even want to use your chart when you have completed it. Place a copy of this in your evidence portfolio.

Line management and colleagues

Organisational structure is important – it lets you know who is in charge of what and who has authority over what. It helps to describe what activities people are responsible for and to whom they are accountable (answerable). Some organisations are *hierarchical*, with many tiers or layers of structure, while others have a *flat* structure and will tend to be less formal. The type of structure of an organisation will to some extent dictate how you interact with your colleagues.

Your particular areas of responsibility and accountability will usually be clearly described in your job description. This document enables you to see what is 'in your own authority' and who your line manager is. The organisational structure enables you to see your role in the wider context of the organisation and will help you identify your relationships with people not only in your immediate area of work but also across the whole organisation.

In many jobs, although you will have your own specific areas of responsibility, you will also be part of a team. You need to be able to work with and support the other members of the team just as they need to be able to work with and support you.

Do you have a job description or, if you are on work placement, a list of activities you will be expected to do? Place a copy in your evidence folder as this is useful as supplementary evidence.

What skills do you need to be able to work as part of a team?

Jason is the receptionist/telephonist at Avits Ltd. The job is located in the administration department and the job holder is responsible to the office manager.

A number of different activities are identified in the job description, including the following:

- Staffing the switchboard – this means that the job holder is usually the first point of contact for any callers to the organisation.

- Greeting visitors to the organisation – the job holder is located in the main reception area of the building.

- Sorting and distributing the incoming mail to all departments.

- Stamping, or franking, and sending out the outgoing mail.

- Word processing of some general correspondence – this is usually to provide support to any of the administrative and secretarial staff in the organisation when their workload is high.

1 Which of these tasks do not affect anyone else's ability to do his or her job (if any)?

2 Which of these tasks may *directly* affect someone else's ability to do his or her job?

3 Which of these activities may *indirectly* affect someone else's ability to do his or her job?

4 What personal attributes and skills do you think someone would need to do this job well?

Now think about your work. Can you identify those activities in your job which you would list under 1, 2 and 3?

Working with colleagues

In almost every type of job, you need to work with others. To do this successfully, it is important to consider how you communicate with all sorts of people. The way you discuss a particular task or problem will be different when you are talking to your line manager, to a colleague in your section with whom you often have lunch, to others in the department with whom you are less likely to socialise, and to the person you are doing the work for (the customer).

The type of organisation you work for will have an influence upon the way you communicate and particularly the degree of formality that is expected. In an organisation with a hierarchical structure, communications systems will tend to be formal, with a greater emphasis on structured written communications such as forms, memos, e-mails and letters. In an organisation with a flatter structure many communications will be much less formal, and while there will still be a need for some records to be kept, there is often a greater use of verbal methods such as telephone and face-to-face conversation. The actual language used will also reflect the degree of formality in the organisation – the tone and structure will be different.

However, whatever the organisation's structure, you will usually need to adjust your style for a range of types of communications. Each of the following will require a different approach:

- seeking advice;
- clarifying requirements;
- sending notification of completion;
- alerting people to delays or problems;
- requesting agreement to proposals; and
- asking for assistance.

Case study: Avits Ltd

You work as the administration assistant in the administration department. The sales manager wishes to introduce a new logging system to record all the telephone sales. You have been asked to draw up a logging sheet and to circulate it to the staff in the sales department by tomorrow.

1 In order to get this task completed in time you will need to ask your colleague, the secretary to the directors, Jan Watts, to help with the weekly filing. As Jan is not in the office until lunch time, write a brief note asking for her assistance.

2 Write a draft memo to be sent to all the staff in the sales department informing them of the new system and asking for their comments on the proposed form. Also draft a memo with similar information to be sent to the two partners of the company.

3 Send a memo to the sales manager, Peter Secunda, alerting him to the possibility of the system being delayed if staff in his department are unable to respond quickly to your request for comments. Include in the memo a request to confirm the contents of the logging sheet.

Discuss with your tutor the differences in tone and structure that are appropriate in these communications.

Handling disagreements and conflicts

Wherever you are, but particularly in your work, there will be times when you have to deal with or work for someone whom you would not have chosen as a friend. However, you do need to be able to carry out your duties and get along. What you need is a strategy to be able to complete your work without upset to you or your colleagues. It is important to make sure that you take into account the implications of how you react and respond to disagreements and conflicts without allowing yourself to be taken advantage of.

You should consider ways of establishing constructive working relationships. You should make sure that you are aware of the 'politics' of the office, taking account of pressures that others might be under and assisting, while ensuring that your workload does not suffer.

Case study: Scorpion Business Solutions

Lauren works in the sales department of a computer company providing administrative support.

Below is a list of difficult situations – some of them are with a colleague, some with a manager and others with a 'customer' (*remember*, it is likely that many of the tasks that you do are for other people).

1 Lauren has word processed a document for a colleague because there was a tight deadline to meet. The task has been completed in time and has been given to the colleague with the printouts ready for mailing. Her colleague has now come back and complained that page 14 of the 20-page document is missing.

2 Lauren has been asked by her manager to look up details in a customer file but the name of the customer has been misspelled in the request. Lauren has sent a note to say that there is no such customer on the computer system and her manager has said that she should have tried several spellings to find it.

3 Lauren has been asked to create a document with the company logo at the top. The requirement is that the document must fit on to one page and that the size of the logo be reduced to ensure this. Lauren has explained that the quality of the resulting logo in the document is poor because of the resolution of the printer but has been told that this is not acceptable.

4 At 4.30 p.m. Lauren is given a complex spreadsheet to create. It is needed by 'the end of the day' but she has noticed that the date on the request is the day before yesterday.

5 It is Friday afternoon and Lauren's manager has already left for the weekend. A customer phones up with a complaint and insists quite rudely that she has been overcharged due to incompetence and wants a commitment to resolve the problem immediately.

In each situation, should Lauren:

a bite her tongue and 'scream' about it later in private;

b discuss the problem calmly but making it clear that she believes she is right;

c tell the person concerned he or she doesn't know what he or she is talking about and can see the manager if he or she has a problem; or

d complete the task grudgingly and make a formal complaint later?

You might find it useful to discuss your answers with your colleagues in the workplace or your manager or supervisor.

Organisation standards

Every organisation has rules about the way it operates. These rules are not simply the ones that are written down in your contract of employment or your college student agreement, but include the rules and conventions that enable the organisation and the people within it to function effectively, efficiently and happily. They can cover everything from the size and font of business communications to the type of dress code expected. So that an organisation can function as one body, it is necessary to define standards to which all staff will work. You may think that 15-point Gothic is the ideal typeface for correspondence, but if your organisation prefers 12-point Times, 12-point Times is what you should use! There will be some areas where there is room for you to use your own initiative, others where you do what your manager or supervisor demands. Part of being at work is learning to identify those situations where you can use your own judgement, those where you need to persuade a more senior colleague of the value of implementing a new idea, and those where you accept the status quo without question.

Information handling

Almost everything you do in your work will involve working with some form of information, e.g. you may be preparing documents, entering data into the computer, answering the telephone, organising a meeting and so on. One of the most important aspects of information handling is that you ensure as far as you can that the information is *correct* and *timely*.

The section on working with data looks particularly at ensuring the correctness of the data as it is processed in a computer system (see page 151). All the activities that take place away from the computer also need to be considered.

In a task such as taking messages, there are a number of steps you can take to make sure that you have done everything necessary to pass on the information.

Case study: Scorpion Business Solutions

Lauren has received the following messages. How should each one be handled to make sure that it is accurate and reaches its destination, taking into account the nature of the message?

1 There is a telephone message for the manager's secretary giving details of the postponement of a meeting this afternoon.

2 A note has been left by a customer for a colleague about a change to an order.

3 There is a fax from one of the sales representatives about a competitor's product promotion starting next week.

4 A phone call has been received for the payroll officer giving bank details for a new member of staff.

5 Just as Lauren's manager was going out of the door, she asked Lauren to phone her business partner to remind him about the meeting at 8.30 tomorrow morning. However, there is no reply.

Discuss your answers with your tutor.

Confidential information

Some of the information that you will be working with will probably be confidential. Almost all organisations have data that should not be freely available to anyone. There will be many different reasons why information is considered to be confidential. Some aspects of confidentiality of data are covered by legislation. Refer to the section on the Data Protection Act (see page 9); *remember*, almost all *personal* data held in an organised form, paper-based or electronic, is covered by this legislation.

There are, however, many other reasons for not giving unrestricted access to information. Most organisations will store, in one form or another, large quantities of information about their own business. This will probably include details regarding financial viability, share of the market in terms of sales and customers, products and services and research and development plans.

In some organisations there is a great deal of effort put into maintaining the confidentiality of information while it is in the computer system, with elaborate password systems and controls on access to the data. However, once the information is printed on paper the level of security often drops.

Do you have:

- secure printing facilities;
- shredders;
- secure fax facilities;
- confidential internal postal systems;
- secure e-mail; and/or
- restricted access to any common pools of documents?

Remember, as an employee it is your duty *not* to discuss your employer's business details with anyone else.

Personal development

What computers are used for and the way they are used are constantly changing. This means that most people who use computers in their work need to be continuously updating their skills just to stay in the same place. Every few months there seems to be yet another release of the software that you use, a bigger, faster processor, etc., and, of course, with this comes the need to relearn the skills you already have. Yet, ideally, what you should be trying to do is *increase* your skills level rather than simply staying still.

In many organisations the main responsibility for ensuring that staff skills are current rests in the first instance with the employees. Many managers prefer their staff to come to them with *solutions* to problems not just the problems themselves. In the context of training and retraining, your manager will want you to know what skills you need and how you intend to get them!

You should consider the following:

- How do you ensure that your skills are current?
- Are there training opportunities available to you through your workplace?
- Where would you like to be in a year's time?

CHECK IT YOURSELF

Draw up a development plan for yourself. You may well be able to use this as the basis for negotiations in discussions with your supervisor or your tutor. What should you include in this plan? A current skills analysis is usually a good place to start – try to do this against the tasks identified in your job description.

Current skills analysis

1 List the tasks that you do regularly and do effectively.

2 List the tasks that you think you could do better if you had additional training.

3 List the tasks that you *need* to be able to do but don't yet have the skills.

4 List the tasks that you would *like* to be able to do but don't yet have the skills for.

5 Identify how each of these would benefit the organisation.

6 Identify how each of these would benefit you and your future.

7 Identify which of these you could 'explore' and start to learn for yourself.

8 Identify which of these would require some training to be provided.

You should now prioritise your list:

1 Put in order of greatest need from those in 2 and 3 above.

2 Put in order of most likely benefit to the organisation those in 4.

3 Choose one that you could 'explore' and one in which you need training from each of these new lists.

4 Put all of this information into a simple report for your supervisor or tutor.

The next step is to take your report forward with your supervisor or tutor. Arrange an appointment with him or her to discuss it (supply a copy of the report *before* the meeting so that your supervisor or tutor has had time to consider what you are proposing).

One way to help you identify what skills you have, and what further skills you need to acquire, is to look at job advertisements. They will often help you to set goals for the future and to decide what skills and personal training might help you achieve them.

CHECK IT YOURSELF

In the appendix 'Applying for a job' (see page 156), there are five job advertisements. Read through them and choose one that you might be interested in working towards, even if you do not have all the necessary skills and experience at the moment.

What additional training would you need to prepare yourself for this job? Make a list. How might you acquire these skills? Are there courses at your local college? What books might be of use? Is it possible for you to get training in the workplace?

Finding your way around

Using a computer system in a working environment should normally enable you to work more efficiently and effectively. If the task you have to do is more time consuming on the computer or does not produce better results than a manual system, then you are probably not making full use of the system's capabilities.

As you become more experienced with the system, you will be able to develop techniques and skills on your own. Today's hardware and software have many features that will assist you with this. Often the best way to find out about these is to explore. Software is usually provided with a booklet which helps you to get started with the software. Most software will also have some form of online help facility, and this can be a good starting point for your exploration. There are few systems today that can be damaged by exploring in this way.

In addition, many software packages are supplied with an online tutorial which will take you through some of these procedures step by step. If you are not sure what you are doing you should seek advice from your supervisor or tutor or refer to a manual.

CHECK IT YOURSELF

Select one software package that you know fairly well and use for a variety of tasks. Do you have access to a supplier's reference manual? Have you been provided with other written information on how to use it? Does it have an online help facility? Do you have an online tutorial for this software? Enter these details in the enhancements checklist on page 96.

Online help

Many software suppliers now supply an online help facility (Figure 22) as the main source of information for the user. One of the main advantages of using the online help system is that you can call it up on to your screen as and when you need it. However, a word of warning: not all these help systems are very helpful and many do not contain every detail about the software.

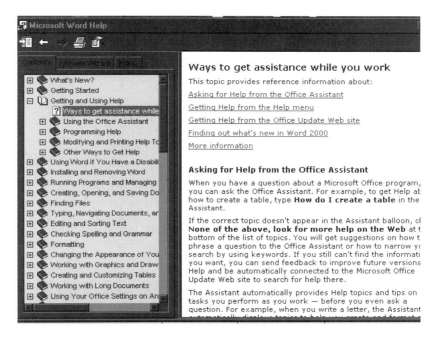

Figure 22 *Online help facility*

There are several different ways to use the online help. For the 'expert user' the index will usually be the most useful section. This provides an interactive, alphabetical listing of all the help available. The contents are organised into a number of sections, usually presented in a sequence in which a new user or relatively novice user may wish to access help. It will usually include a section called 'getting started' which will provide the basic information on how to use the software. There will also be a section telling you about the different ways of getting help. Using the contents can be very useful if you do not know exactly what you are looking for, or for browsing when you want to learn something new.

Online helper

A useful feature of many help facilities is an online helper. This assistant can provide information on keywords that the user types in or in response to a question. For example, 'How do I print envelopes?' may well offer you information on how to create and print envelopes, troubleshoot printing envelopes, customise envelopes size, etc. This helper can also be called upon as you are carrying out a task, and will make a guess as to the kind of help you might need.

Internet-based help

Many software online help facilites will also provide a direct link to the supplier's web site. Here you will often get useful tips and techniques that many of the supplier's customers have asked about; there will usually be a FAQ (frequently asked questions) section which may well have the answer you need. There will also be the opportunity to get up-to-date information about new features and to download updates and other files such as additional 'clip-art'.

Other help

In many organisations, simple information sheets have been produced for frequently used features of a piece of software. These can be very useful as they are usually written by users, not computer experts, and often will be more 'user friendly'. There is also a wide range of commercially produced books and quick reference guides for the more commonly used software packages. These are very useul for those who know how to use the software but need something to refer to, particularly for commands they do not use very often.

CHECK IT YOURSELF

Does any of the software you use offer Internet-based help? If you have access to the Internet, find out what sort of help is available. Does the organisation where you work provide information sheets? Where are they available from, and would any be of help to you? (You could include details of these in your evidence portfolio.) Record details of these in the enhancements checklist on page 96).

Enhancements checklist

Name of software package	
Supplier's reference manual?	Yes ☐ No ☐
Is the manual 'user friendly'?	Yes ☐ No ☐
Written user instructions?	Yes ☐ No ☐
Online help facility?	Yes ☐ No ☐
Online tutorial?	Yes ☐ No ☐

How useful is the online help?

How useful is the online help assistant?

Internet-based help?	Yes ☐ No ☐

What sort of help is available via the Internet?

Information sheets?	Yes ☐ No ☐

Which sheets are of most use to you?

OPTIONAL UNITS

Unit 202 Produce Documents Using Word Processing Software

This unit contains three elements:

202.1 Retrieve and enter data to create and update files
202.2 Produce the required documents by manipulating data
202.3 Output the document to the required destination.

You need to demonstrate that you can identify and correctly interpret your customer's requirements. You will also need to show that you can work effectively with word processing software to create, retrieve, edit, format and output documents as required.

To meet the requirements of this unit, you should have a good basic understanding of the range of word processing features and functions necessary to produce documents and the factors that will influence your choice to meet a specific requirement. You should understand the importance of accuracy and the checking facilities available within the software, the different output devices available and issues of confidentiality when producing this output.

What is word processing?

Word processing is the term used to describe the computer-based production of text-based documents.

When producing such documents, you will usually be working to the requirements of your manager, colleague or other 'customer'. You will be required to produce these documents to meet their standards both in terms of 'house style' and general layout and presentation, and within the time scales they define.

In most organisations, letters, internal communications such as memos, forms and reports are prepared using some form of electronic text processing facility, usually a word processing system. Modern word processing facilities have features way beyond those that would have previously been carried out on a typewriter. Many documents are now produced in-house that would have been sent out to specialist designers and printers in the past, or may have been created through the use of more specialist software such as desktop publishing (DTP).

The basic text processing facilities of wordwrap, editing, cutting and pasting and tabulation have been greatly enhanced with a wide range of features such as the ability to carry out automatic numbering of paragraphs, use bullets, apply spell checkers in a variety of languages, look up words in a thesaurus to assist in the use of just the right word and sophisticated line drawing and text presentation features.

Many of the uses of word processing, such as filling in forms, can be automated through the use of interactive macros which assist the user by prompting at each point in the process. Mailmerge facilities mean that standard mailings can be prepared easily for multiple recipients but with each having the look and presentation of individual correspondence.

The major advances in the quality and economy of printing have made many of these features possible. Laser and colour ink-jet printers are available for desktop use and can produce output which is close to the quality that was once available only on expensive printing equipment. To support this, word processing software offers a wide range of fonts and text enhancements to enable the user to produce impressive looking documents.

Document production

Presentation of data: document layout

Whatever kind of document you are producing, a whole range of layout and presentation decisions need to be made. Although there will be slightly different ways of achieving these layout effects, most modern word processing, database, spreadsheet and desktop publishing packages will enable you to control the presentation of your documents.

The page

Depending on your printer and its ability to handle different sizes of paper, you will be able to select the following:

- *Paper size.* If you are using a laser printer or ink-jet printer it will usually be A4 (210 × 297 mm or 8.27 × 11.69 in) but may also be Legal (8.5 × 14 in) or Letter (8.5 × 11 in). You may also be able to print on a range of different sizes of envelopes and other specialist stationery.

- *Paper orientation.* Most printers are able to handle printing on the paper in either portrait or landscape (see Figure 23).

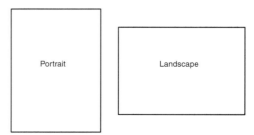

Figure 23 *Paper orientation*

- *Margins.* The usable area of the page on which you can place the main part of your document is controlled by setting the size of the four margins – top, bottom, left and right (see Figure 24).

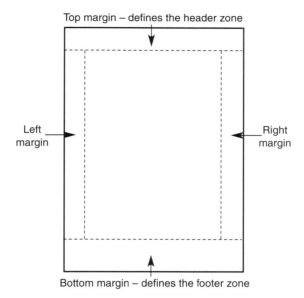

Top margin – defines the header zone

Left margin

Right margin

Bottom margin – defines the footer zone

Figure 24 *Page margins*

- *Headers and footers.* A header is text that appears in the header zone defined by the top margin. It appears at the top of every page. A footer is text that appears in the footer zone defined by the bottom margin. It appears at the bottom of every page. Headers and footers can be set up so that they are different for odd and even pages of a document or different on the first page of a document. It is also possible to have a number of different sections to your document and for the header or footer to change for each section.
- *Best fit.* This is a facility which can be used automatically to adjust the layout and presentation of the document so that the information can all be fitted on to the page or into a given area of the page.
- *Footnote.* A footnote is text which is referenced in the main body of the document, often using a number, and then either printed at the bottom of the page or at the end of a section.
- *Page numbering.* The software will usually let you specify whether you want the pages of a document to be numbered automatically and where this should be printed, in the header or the footer. You will also be able to include such controls as omitting the number on page 1, something you often wish to do particularly with letters, and starting to count the pages from any number. This is useful where the document is only part of the final product.

- *Date/time stamping.* It is often very useful for a document to have the date and/or time that it was created or last updated printed automatically, usually as part of a header or footer.

The paragraph

- *Justification.*

This is an example of *left*-justified text. The left margin is aligned but the right margin is ragged.	This is an example of *right*-justified text. The right margin is aligned but the left margin is ragged.	This an example of text that has *full* justification. Both the left and the right margins are aligned. It is achieved by the software spreading the text to fit the margins by inserting additional *soft* spaces.

- *Lines and boxes.* There will often be a range of ways in which you can highlight and draw attention to parts of a document. You will be able to draw lines and boxes and, even if you don't have colour printing facilities, you can using shading and patterns to produce a variety of effects.

The text

- *Font style.* The shape and style of the text can be varied enormously. Most printers will support a considerable number of fonts. Some are very plain and clear and therefore appropriate for business applications, while others are much more fancy and elaborate (*like this one which is called Brush Script*) and are very effective for less formal communications or possibly for posters and leaflets.
- *Font size.* Not only can you use different fonts, but you can also control the size. With printers capable of producing very high-quality print, it is not only possible to print very small, fine characters quite clearly but also to print very large letters. Most fonts are measured in points – the bigger the number, the larger the character.
- *Text enhancements.* As well as enhancing the way the text looks by using different fonts and sizes, it also possible to add emphasis to selected parts of the text. The three most commonly used forms of emphasis are **emboldening**, *italics* and underlining. It is, of course, possible to use a combination of these features to achieve different effects.

However, it is extremely important that you use these features appropriately and not excessively. Too many different types of enhancement and emphasis within the same document will only cause confusion and detract from the content.

House styles

So that an organisation can have control of its image – the way it presents itself to the outside world – it is usual for certain rules and guidelines to be laid down about external communications. At its most basic level, this will probably include an organisation standard on how letters are to be laid out. Further to this, to maintain and foster a corporate identity, it is also quite normal to have rules and guidelines for internal communications.

Most organisations will have some form of logo, often based upon the name of the organisation and usually incorporating a graphic or image. These days this will often be held as a graphic file which is readily available to all computer users so that it can be incorporated into documents.

In some organisations there will be a set of guidelines as to which fonts and sizes are to used for particular situations; in others, documents will be less formalised. There may be a different set of guidelines for in-house and external communications.

Letter layout

Something as apparently simple as how a letter is laid out is important for an organisation's image. There are many different ways of presenting a letter, and 'normal' practice changes. Quite often the changes are in response to the latest facilities available in the most recent release of the word processing software. For example, until word processors became commonplace, the justification of text could not be controlled easily and so text was almost always left aligned. With the general availability of high-quality laser printers with a range of fonts and sizes, the way text is emphasised has changed. For example, <u>underlining</u> of text is far less popular than a few years ago, whereas the use of *italics* or **bold** is often preferred.

How do you write the date, and where is it placed? Most word processing systems are capable of inserting the current date automatically (or at least the date the computer calculates it to be!) and you can choose its format. Commonly used date formats include:

06/05/00; 06 May 2000; 6 May 2000; May 6 2000; 6-May-00

You should note, however, that conventions differ in the USA, so a letter from there dated 06/05/00 would indicate it was written on 5 June 2000!

Pages of documents may be numbered automatically and you can decide whereabouts on the page to place the numbers and what they should look like. Some organisations like to have a standard where the first page of a letter does not have a number (so a single-page letter will not be numbered) whereas others will include a page number on page 1 if there is more than one page. For letters, it is usual to have page numbers somewhere in the footer of the page, either on the left, right or in the centre.

Which font and size should you use? There will usually be a preferred, or even required, style. One thing is certain, however: above all else you must ensure that you are *consistent*.

You should make sure you know the organisation's conventions on:

- use of letterheads;
- addressing conventions;
- bold/underlining, etc.;
- paragraphs – justification/blocks;
- page numbering; and
- date format and position (see Figure 25).

Figure 25 *House style*

There will probably be a similar, although possibly less formal, requirement for internal communications such as memos.

Layout of reports

Again, there will probably be some conventions in the organisation for the production of reports. They will, as with letters, be based upon consistency and the image the organisation wishes to present, and will probably include the following:

- Section and paragraph numbering systems. Most word processors enable you to number paragraphs automatically with a range of different systems to choose from (a, b, c, or i, ii, iii, or 1, 2, 3, etc.).
- Justification of paragraphs – this may depend upon whom the report is for and whether it is to be circulated internally only, or also to be distributed externally.
- Page numbering – as with letters there is a range of options. Reports may have the page numbers at the top or the bottom of the page and will often identify how many pages there are in total (e.g. Page 1 of 5).
- Drafts – how should the draft status of a document be indicated? For example, the word 'draft' may be included as part of a header, or it may appear as a 'watermark' across each page, and may be in capitals. Many organisations print reports in double-line spacing while they are in draft format, so that revisions can be more easily indicated. Sometimes revisions are retained between drafts, using features such as strikethrough and margin lines, so that they are visible until the final document.
- A date – this may appear on every page, usually in the header or footer.

Word processing features

Whichever word processing software you are using, you will need to be familiar with all the standard features and many of the advanced facilities offered.

Text format

In addition to the format features outlined above, there are many facilities offered by your word processing software to improve the appearance of your documents and/or to enable you to achieve high-quality documents more easily.

There are many occasions when a document will contain a list of items. Sometimes these will need to have some form of numbering system attached to them to indicate their sequence. The most effective way of achieving this is to use the automatic numbering feature available in the software. This will then enable the numbers to be updated automatically if you need to add/delete items to/from your list. There will be a range of systems available, including single level (a, b, c or 1, 2, 3, etc.) and multi-level systems (1, 1.1, 1.2, 1.3, 2, 2.1, 2.2, or 1, a, b, c, 2, a, b, c, etc.).

However, not all lists should be numbered. Some lists will not indicate an order, merely that all items should be included. A system of 'bullets' is then available. These are symbols that indicate the start of each new item in the list and will most frequently take the form of a dot (•), although almost any symbol can be used. It is also possible for these lists to be multi-level, e.g. a different bullet shape or a dash being used for each level.

The spaces between the lines of text are a very important presentation feature in any document. In most types of documents it is usual to have an additional line space between each paragraph. Until recently, this was most frequently achieved by putting in an additional return. However, it is now better to control the amount of space above and/or below each paragraph by setting this in the paragraph format facility. You can also change the spacing between the lines of text by adjusting the line spacing. In many word processing packages this will include single, double and 1.5 line spacing.

When creating a complex document, with a number of different paragraph formats, e.g. headings, subheadings, main text and notes text, you can define each one as a *paragraph style* specifying the font, size, indents, justification, paragraph and line spacing, etc. You then apply the paragraph style required, thus achieving a consistent format. If you decide to change the format of the document, you need only amend the style definition and re-apply it throughout the document.

Tabulation is available to help you align columns of information within your document. You will usually be able to do this by placing *tabs* in the required positions on a ruler. These tabs can be set for left, right, centre or decimal alignment depending on the type of data to be included and it may also be possible to include a *leader*, usually a series of dots, to draw a line up to the column of data. This could be used, for example, when producing a contents page with page numbers.

Another facility to enable you to produce columns of information is the *tables* feature. This is particularly useful when each block of data in a column needs to occupy more than one line. You can also include a range of borders, grid lines and shading to improve the presentation of your tables.

Text manipulation

One of the many benefits of word processing is that, once some text has been entered, you can modify it until it is as required. You can delete unwanted text, either as individual characters or as a block of text. You can add new text either by overtyping, replacing what is already there, or by inserting it exactly where it is needed, moving the rest of the text to accommodate it. You can move a block of text from one part of the document to another by a process usually known as 'cut and paste', and you can copy any part of the text, retaining the original while placing the copy where it is required.

An extremely useful editing facility – *find and replace* – will enable you to find all the occurrences of an item of text (it could be a word, a phrase or even a sentence) and replace each instance with alternative text.

Most word processing packages offer a *sort* facility whereby you can organise items of information in a list of ascending or descending order, either numerically or alphabetically. This feature is usually found within the tables facility (see above). You will usually be able to sort the information in a table based upon the order of one or more of the columns. For example, if you word processed a list of staff with their internal telephone extension numbers, the list would be far more useful presented in alphabetical order of name so that you could find the number you needed more quickly.

There will be times when information contained within one document needs to be included in another. In these cases, the *insert file* facility makes a copy of the original document and transfers it to the one you are working on. This can be extremely useful, for example, if a number of people are involved in the production of a large document – each can work in separate files which can be merged together into one file when completed – or where a standard piece of text may need to be included in a number of different documents.

The word processing checklist on page 110 includes all the main text manipulation features that you will need to be able to use in your particular software. As you progress through the qualification, complete section 5 so that you can include this in your evidence folder as supplementary evidence.

Graphical manipulation – integration of text, data and images

Many documents, either for business or leisure purposes, can be improved and enhanced by the use of graphics or the inclusion of a set of data. A general newsletter distributed to all staff is more interesting to look at if it includes more than words; company reports are quicker to produce if the tables or figures do not need to be typed in again and can also be displayed as a graph; the invitation for all staff to the interdepartmental five-a-side football match will be more inviting with some pictures in it (see Figure 26).

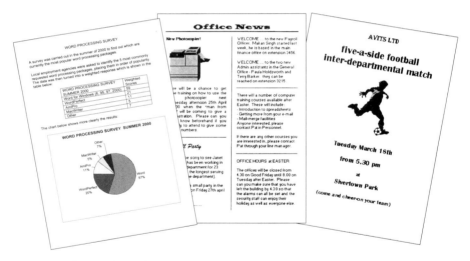

Figure 26 *Graphics enhance text*

Recently, there have been considerable advances in the capability of software to help you integrate text, data and graphics within a document. Previously, it was usually necessary to use specialist software such as a desktop publishing package in order to incorporate graphical images into a text document. In most instances, these packages required a high level of specialist skills in order to achieve high-quality presentations. Now, most word processing packages have the capability of handling graphics in almost any format and have made this presentation form accessible to all.

At the same time as software developments have been taking place, advances in the power of computers have kept pace. Many desktop computers are now capable of simulating 'multi-tasking'. This means that although you can only use one package at a time, it is possible to have a number of packages loaded into the computer's memory and for the user to 'switch' between them. With the ability to have a number of different applications open at the same time, the process of passing data between them has become much quicker. This is usually achieved by using a facility often known as the *clipboard*. This is a part of the RAM that is set aside as a special storage area. You can place a *copy* of the data, images, etc., on to it and then *paste* this into another document or file.

For example, you are creating a simple set of instructions for your colleagues on how to run the new software that has been set up. You want to include in your word processed document a 'screen-shot', or picture of the screen, to improve the clarity of your description:

- When working in Windows, you can take a 'screen-shot' by pressing the Print Screen key. This places a copy of the image of the screen on the clipboard.
- Then, with the word processing document open, you can paste this image from the clipboard into the document.

Note: in many instances, whatever has been placed on the clipboard will remain there until you replace it with something else, or close down the system.

All modern word processing packages include the capability to include images within documents. You need to be able to insert images from a variety of sources and ensure that these images are placed where required. You will also be expected to be able to change the size of the image to fit the document appropriately. When you change the size of an image it is extremely important that you do not distort the image – you do not want an elongated version of the image nor one that is foreshortened (see Figure 27).

      Original   Elongated   Foreshortened

Figure 27 *Original and distorted images*

CHECK IT YOURSELF

The word processing checklist on page 110 includes all the main graphical manipulation features you will need to be able to use in your particular word processing software. As you progress through the qualification, complete section 6 so that you can include this in your evidence folder as supplementary evidence.

Organisation house styles checklist

Section 1: the letter	
Organisation letterhead	Yes ☐ No ☐
Preprinted stationery?	Yes ☐ No ☐
Available as a graphical image?	Yes ☐ No ☐
Specified font and size	Font: Size:
Page numbering convention	
Date format and position	
Emphasis	
Paragraphs – justification/blocks	
Section 2: the memo	
Standard format	Yes ☐ No ☐
Preprinted stationery	Yes ☐ No ☐
Specified font and size	Font: Size:
Date format	
References – footers	
Section 3: formal reports	
Standard format	Yes ☐ No ☐
Specified font and size	Font: Size:
Paragraph numbering systems	
Paragraph formats – justification	
Page numbering	
Draft layouts, e.g. line spacing	
Headers and footers	
Date formats	

Word processing checklist

Section 1: text formatting functions

Appearance	Different fonts	☐
	Size of text	☐
	Bold	☐
	Italics	☐
	Underlining	☐
	Other	☐
Margins	Left and right	☐
	Top and bottom	☐
	Header and footer	☐
Indent	Left and right	☐
	Hanging	☐
	First line of paragraph	☐
Tabs	Left	☐
	Right	☐
	Centre	☐
	Decimal	☐
	Leaders	☐
Paragraphs	Justification	☐
	Line spacing	☐
	Text flow	☐

Section 2: document layout

Page layout	Page size	☐
	Page orientation	☐
Page numbering	Positioning	☐
	First page	☐
	Format	☐
	Start value	☐

Word processing checklist (continued)

Headers and footers	First page	☐
	Alternate page	☐
	New sections	☐
	Footnotes	☐
Columns	Newspaper	☐
	Parallel	☐
Presentation	Lines	☐
	Boxes	☐
Section 3: document structure		
Directories	Indexing	☐
	Table of contents	☐
Paragraph numbering	Numbers	☐
	Bullets	☐
	Multilevel	☐
Section 4: other facilities		
Data checking	Spell checker	☐
	Thesaurus	☐
	Print preview	☐
Section 5: text manipulation		
Modifications	Delete	☐
	Insert	☐
	Move – cut and paste	☐
	Copy	☐
	Find and replace	☐
Insert	Text document	☐
	Structured data	☐
	Numerical models	☐
	Merge documents	☐
	Sort text	☐

Word processing checklist (continued)

Section 6: graphical manipulation		
Modifications	Change size	☐
	Re-position	☐
	Crop	☐
Insert into text-based documents	Images – ClipArt	☐
	Images – other	☐
	Graphical displays	☐

Unit 203 Produce Spreadsheet Documents

This unit contains three elements:

203.1 Retrieve and enter data to create and update files
203.2 Produce the required spreadsheet by manipulating data
203.3 Output the spreadsheet to the required destination.

You need to demonstrate that you can identify and correctly interpret your customer's requirements. You will also need to show that you can work effectively with spreadsheet software to create, retrieve, edit, format and output spreadsheet documents as required. This will include working with numerical data and applying relevant and appropriate calculations as required.

To meet the requirements of this unit, you will need to have a good basic understanding of the range of spreadsheet features and functions necessary to produce numerical models and the factors that will influence your choice to meet a specific requirement. You should understand the importance of accuracy and the checking facilities available within the software, the different output devices available and issues of confidentiality when producing this output.

What is a spreadsheet?

One of the things computers have always been used for is to carry out calculations. They are capable of carrying out vast numbers of calculations in a very short space of time. Many of these applications involve the use of special software which has been set up to perform specific functions such as accounting, complex engineering design calculations, production forecasting or even putting humans on the moon. However, we all need to be able to do much simpler calculations, both in our daily lives and in our work.

Most spreadsheets look like the one shown in Figure 28.

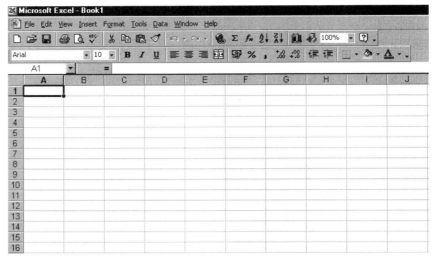

Figure 28 *A typical spreadsheet layout*

It is like a very large piece of paper that is divided into columns and rows. What you can see on the screen at any one time is just a small part of the complete spreadsheet available. The screen is like a small window on to the complete spreadsheet. If you try to move the cursor off the edge of the screen, then a new portion of the spreadsheet comes into view but you do not lose the data in the part that is no longer displayed. When you scroll back, the data will still be there.

Each entry position in the spreadsheet is called a *cell* and you can reference any particular cell by giving its column *letter* followed by the row *number*, e.g. D4.

The selection border around the first cell on the worksheet tells you that this is the active cell. This is the cell that will be affected by your next entry.

In the upper left part of your screen the cell reference shows the number of the cell you are working in at the moment, the active cell. In Figure 28, it is A1 because the selected cell is located in column A, row 1.

Each cell can contain one item of data which can be:

- *text* – any character;
- *numeric* – only real numbers should be entered as numeric; or
- *formulae* – to perform calculations.

Calculations, using formulae, can be entered into a cell. These may use the contents of other cells or absolute values. When the values in a cell are changed, all the formulae in the spreadsheet are automatically recalculated to give new results.

Producing a spreadsheet model

We all know how difficult it is to keep track of our money and make sure that there will be enough to meet our commitments. To do this, using pen and paper, you would probably make a list of all the sources of money coming in, your pay cheques, benefits or grant, and then make another list of all your regular expenditure. You would probably want to look at this over a period of time, say four weeks, and so you might end up with something like Figure 29.

MY PERSONAL MONTHLY BUDGET				
	WEEK 1	WEEK 2	WEEK 3	WEEK 4
BALANCE IN MONEY IN Wages Other MONEY OUT Rent Electricity Food etc Entertainment Clothes Travel Other				
TOTAL IN TOTAL OUT BALANCE				

Figure 29 *Layout for a monthly budget*

You would then need to write down all the amounts of money, carry out all the necessary calculations (adding up and subtracting), possibly using a calculator. But then, what if you realised that you'd left something out, over- or under-estimated how much something cost, or just added it up wrongly? Your piece of paper could end up looking like Figure 30.

MY PERSONAL MONTHLY BUDGET

	WEEK 1	WEEK 2	WEEK 3	WEEK 4
BALANCE IN	21.23	60.93	130.63	−29.67
MONEY IN				
Wages	155.00	155.00	155.00	155.00
Other		30.00	30.00	
MONEY OUT				
Rent			225.00	
Electricity	5.00	5.00	5.00	5.00
Food etc	30.00	30.00	30.00	30.00
Entertainment	15.00 10.00	15.00	15.00	15.00
Clothes	30.00 10.00	5.00	30 40.00	20
Travel	20.30	20.30	20.30	20.30
Other	15.00	5 10.00	15.00	15.00
TOTAL IN	176.23 155.00	215.93	315 283.63	125.33 55.00
TOTAL OUT	115.30	85.30	345.30	85.30
BALANCE	60.93	130.63	−29.67	40.03

Figure 30 *A worked-out monthly budget*

A spreadsheet package will do all these things for you, and you can keep changing it until it is right.

When you were trying to solve your problem using a piece of paper and a pencil, the first step was to draw up a layout showing the column and row headings that you needed. You included in this spaces for the results of your calculations (see Figure 29). When you are using a spreadsheet you need to do exactly the same; you should decide what column and row headings you require.

The next step in the paper and pencil method was to put the numerical data in the rows and columns (see Figure 30). Again, you should do exactly the same when using a spreadsheet.

Finally, you carried out the calculations and put the results in the appropriate columns and rows on your sheet of paper. With a spreadsheet, you put the formula that will carry out the required calculation into the cell where the result should go (see Figure 31).

	A	B	C	D	E	F
1	My personal monthly budget					
2						
3		WEEK 1	WEEK 2	WEEK 3	WEEK 4	
4	BALANCE IN	21.23	60.93	130.63	-29.67	
5						
6	MONEY IN					
7						
8	Wages	155.00	155.00	155.00	155.00	
9	Other			30.00		
10						
11	MONEY OUT					
12						
13	Rent			225.00		
14	Electricity	5.00	5.00	5.00	5.00	
15	Food etc	30.00	30.00	35.00	30.00	
16	Entertainment	15.00	15.00	15.00	15.00	
17	Clothes	30.00		30.00		
18	Travel	20.30	20.30	20.30	20.30	
19	Other	15.00	15.00	15.00	15.00	
20						
21	TOTAL IN	176.23	215.93	315.63	125.33	
22	TOTAL OUT	115.30	85.30	345.30	85.30	
23						
24	BALANCE	60.93	130.63	-29.67	40.03	
25						

Figure 31 *A set of values – this shows the results of the calculations with one particular set of data*

If you then find that you have made an error in your data, you can change the value and the results will be recalculated automatically.

The formulae, or rules, together with the column and row headings define the *model*. Spreadsheets are often used to create a model which will then be used for many different sets of data. In this situation, you would need to save a copy of the spreadsheet which *only* contained the row and column headings and the formulae, i.e. without any data. This model would also need to be printed showing the formulae so that the model was fully documented and could be used by others (see Figure 32).

	A	B	C	D	E
1	My personal monthly bu dget				
2					
3		WEEK 1	WEEK 2	WEEK 3	WEEK 4
4	BALANCE IN		=B24	=C24	=D24
5					
6	MONEY IN				
7					
8	Wages				
9	Other				
10					
11	MONEY OUT				
12					
13	Rent				
14	Electricity				
15	Food etc				
16	Entertainment				
17	Clothes				
18	Travel				
19	Other				
20					
21	TOTAL IN	=SUM(B4:B9)	=SUM(C4:C9)	=SUM(D4:D9)	=SUM(E4:E9)
22	TOTAL OUT	=SUM(B13:B19)	=SUM(C13:C19)	=SUM(D13:D19)	=SUM(E13:E19)
23					
24	BALANCE	=B21-B22	=C21-C22	=D21-D22	=E21-E22
25					

Figure 32 *The model – this shows the layout with column and row headings and the formulae*

Once you have set up the layout and rules for your calculations, you can enter and edit the numeric data to project results for different situations.

Who uses a spreadsheet? The answer is, almost anyone. A spreadsheet package is often used as a management tool to examine numerical data and to make 'what if' projections. It is used by accountants, sales and marketing executives, personnel departments, project managers and also for many general administrative and clerical tasks. Quite often the data entered into a spreadsheet has been extracted from another computer program (e.g. the accounting software) and then imported into the spreadsheet so that further calculations can be carried out.

As with all modern software, it is also possible to have considerable control over how the information is displayed and printed. You will be able to adjust the orientation of the page, alter the margins so that you get the 'best fit' on the page, include headers and footers, control the justification of the text and apply lots of different types of enhancements such as lines, boxes, bold, italics and use shading to highlight headings or important cells of information. You can also extract all or part of a spreadsheet to be used in another application such as in your word processed report (see the section on integration on page 106).

Because a spreadsheet is very versatile, it is an extremely flexible modelling tool that lends itself to a wide range of uses. All spreadsheet packages work in an almost identical way and have a set of reasonably simple, basic commands you need to be able to use.

However, to create a model that works well, you need to have a clear understanding of the factors to be included and the way in which it will be used. The most effective models are planned before they are entered into a software package. Some preparation at the design stage can significantly reduce the amount of correction needed later. The design of the layout is extremely important. You need to consider:

- the format of the data;
- the information required from the model;
- the calculations and formulae that have to be applied to the data;
- how easy it will be to amend;
- how easy it will be to extract data for another application; and
- the way the results are to be presented.

Spreadsheet features

Whichever spreadsheet software you are using, you will need to be very familiar with all the standard features and many of the advanced facilities offered.

Worksheet manipulation

The structure of a spreadsheet of cells in rows and columns dictates how you move around and manipulate the contents of the sheet. You can select an individual cell as your active cell or you can select a group of cells to work with. This could be an entire row or column, or a selected range of cells, sometimes referred to as a *block*.

You may need to insert an additional row or column in between existing ones. You may need the spreadsheet rows to move down and create an empty row or you may need the column to move across and create an empty column.

Similarly, you may need to delete a row or column. Deleting means not only erasing the data but also closing up the rows or columns so that there is no space left. It is different from the command which leaves the cells in the layout but without any data in them. You should take considerable care when deleting; if you delete the wrong column or row you may not be able to call it back. It is usually a good idea to save your work before deleting, just to be safe.

Often when you are putting data into a spreadsheet, there is a lot of repetition. You can replicate, or copy, the contents of a cell to any other cell by the use of a copy command. You can also use the copy command to copy a formula from one cell to another.

The formula that you used to calculate the TOTAL IN for Week 1 in your personal budget spreadsheet would look something like this:

=SUM(B4:B9)

To add up the TOTAL IN for Week 2, you need a formula that looks like this:

=SUM(C4:C9)

The only difference is that this formula refers to column C rather than column B.

When you copy a formula that looks like this, the software automatically changes the cell references *relative* to where it is being copied to.

You can also use the *cut and paste* feature of a spreadsheet package. However, you must be extremely careful with this. It does not always work in exactly the same way as in other software. For example, if you wish to move the data from column A to column C and column C already has some data in it, the cut and paste facility will *overwrite* the contents of column C unless you insert an additional column to take the moved data.

There may be occasions when you will need to reorganise the order in which the rows of data are presented. Although this a relatively straightforward function, it is one that should be carried out with great care as it is possible to destroy completely the validity of the data in the sheet. It is therefore always sensible to save your work before manipulating it in this way.

The most likely error that will occur is that you will only sort the data in the specified column and the data in the other columns will remain where they were. For example, a spreadsheet with columns containing the names of the staff and their travel expenses for each month could result in the wrong expenses being attributed to the staff (see Figure 33).

TRAVEL EXPENSES FOR SALES DEPARTMENT STAFF							
Name		**January**	**February**	**March**	**April**	**May**	**June**
Kerry	Walker	117.50	106.35	89.24	125.38	111.50	204.00
Julian	Peters	56.23	84.20	78.56	76.00	45.39	48.25
Adrian	Walsh	77.25	115.60	145.63	125.80	106.50	85.25
Gillian	Armstrong	103.50	86.57	46.25	105.36	59.25	85.60
Bella	Epong	102.78	75.60	65.50	89.25	110.25	95.65
Tushar	Patel	46.50	42.30	35.85	57.21	61.30	48.25

a Before the sort

TRAVEL EXPENSES FOR SALES DEPARTMENT STAFF							
Name		**January**	**February**	**March**	**April**	**May**	**June**
Gillian	Armstrong	117.50	106.35	89.24	125.38	111.50	204.00
Bella	Epong	56.23	84.20	78.56	76.00	45.39	48.25
Tushar	Patel	77.25	115.60	145.63	125.80	106.50	85.25
Julian	Peters	103.50	86.57	46.25	105.36	59.25	85.60
Kerry	Walker	102.78	75.60	65.50	89.25	110.25	95.65
Adrian	Walsh	46.50	42.30	35.85	57.21	61.30	48.25

b After the sort

Figure 33 *Can you identify what error has been made here?*

Spreadsheet presentation

Whether you are producing documents using spreadsheet software, word processing software or any other package which results in paper-based output, many of the presentation considerations are the same. You should make sure that you are fully aware of the standards and conventions required by your organisation (see 'House styles' in Unit 202 on page 101).

Many of the layout features are the same; you will need to know how to change the orientation of the page, include headers and footers and adjust the four margins of the page (top, bottom, left and right). You will need to know how to use features such as page numbering and date/time stamping and to achieve 'best fit' for your data.

The spreadsheet checklist on page 125 includes all the main layout features you need to be able to use in your particular software. As you progress through the qualification, complete section 1 so that you can include this in your evidence folder as supplementary evidence.

As a spreadsheet is based on rows and columns, and as much of the data is numeric, it is often quite important to include grid lines to improve the readability of the document. In addition to this, there are a range of border lines and styles available to enhance the presentation. These lines and borders can be used to separate the information into sections and to highlight individual cells or blocks of cells. Additionally, you will usually be able to use colour and shading to improve the final document.

The default display width of a column is usually sufficient to display approximately nine characters. This will vary between packages and where you are working with a proportional spacing font will depend upon the particular characters included. The width of the column only relates to the *display* of the column; you can always put more than nine characters into a cell but they may not all be displayed. The way this non-displayed data is treated depends upon what type of data it is. However, you must remember that because the structure of a spreadsheet is based upon columns, you cannot change the width of a single cell but only the width of the whole column.

If it is *text*, and there is something in the cell next to it, the text will be *truncated* (cut short).

If it is *text*, and the cell next to it is *empty*, it will *continue* into the next cell. (This is very useful for titles at the top of a spreadsheet.)

If it is *numeric* it will often be displayed as a row of ######### to warn you that there is not enough room to display the number; it would be extremely unhelpful if the numbers were truncated – you would often not notice this and the wrong results would be displayed! Sometimes the scientific notation is used; 5.98E+09 is actually 5,980,000,000.

You will need to decide exactly how the data should be displayed, that is, what formats are required. The default display for text data is left aligned within the cell. Sometimes, particularly when used as column headings, it would make the spreadsheet easier to read if the text was displayed as right or centre aligned. You will usually be able to align data over a range of cells so that you could, for example, centre a heading across all the cells it relates to. You may also be able to increase the depth of the row and use wordwrap facilities to include longer text without needing to make the column wider.

The default display for numeric data is right aligned within the cell. This is how numeric data should be aligned; a left or centre-aligned column of figures does not easily display the numerical significance of the numbers and is therefore not useful. However, when you are considering the display of numeric data there are factors to take into account.

When all the numbers you enter are *integers* (whole numbers) the data is displayed in an easily readable format. However, when you enter numbers that include a *decimal point* the spreadsheet does not by default display *non-significant* zeros (except the one immediately preceding the decimal point). For example:

10.00	is displayed as:	10
10.50	is displayed as:	10.5
.45	is displayed as:	0.45
00.342	is displayed as:	0.342
1.868	is displayed as:	1.868

As you can see, although the numbers are right-justified, they are difficult to read as they are not aligned on the decimal point. This default display is known as general format. However, numbers usually need to be displayed to align with the decimal point. You will need to decide the degree of precision that is required. For example, most financial data should be accurate to two places of decimal whereas summary data will usually only be required as whole numbers. The format command will usually be able either to round up or down to the nearest whole number or to ignore the numbers after the decimal point. For example, 0.342 would be rounded down to 0.34 and 1.868 would be rounded up to 1.87. You will be able to include currency and percentage signs within numeric cells and also to define your own formats.

CHECK IT YOURSELF

The spreadsheet checklist on page 125 includes all the main data formatting features you need to be able to use in your particular software. As you progress through the qualification, complete section 2 so that you can include this in your evidence folder as supplementary evidence.

Calculation facilities

The primary reason for using spreadsheets to provide an information technology solution is that they are particularly useful for carrying out calculations. Calculations are achieved in a spreadsheet by placing *formulae* or *functions* into a cell. The results of the calculation are then displayed in the cell and, when any of the data used in the formula is changed, a new result will be calculated.

You will need to make sure that you know how to include formulae to carry out addition, subtraction, multiplication and division. The arithmetic operators use the following keys:

Addition	+
Subtraction	-
Multiplication	*
Division	/

Any formula can include reference to any cell or block of cells in the spreadsheet and it may also include absolute values – see, for example, Figure 34.

Cell	Formula	What it does
B15	=B7+B12	Adds the value in B7 to the value in B12 and displays the result in B15
C15	=C10-C11	Subtracts the value in C11 from the value in C10 and displays the result in C15
D15	=D13*D14	Multiplies the value in D13 by the value in D14 and displays the result in D15
E15	=E8/E9	Divides the value in E8 by the value in E9 and displays the result in E15
F15	=F3*5	Multiplies the value in F3 by the absolute value 5 and displays the result in F15

Figure 34 *Examples of formulae*

The formulae that you use may look slightly different from the examples shown in Figure 34 depending upon which software package you are using, but will be similar.

Some of the calculations that are used most frequently in a spreadsheet will have a function predefined to make it easier and quicker to do. The most commonly used calculation in a spreadsheet is to add up a column or row of data. A function exists in your spreadsheet known as the SUM function. This function provides a formula that adds up the values in every cell within the range given. For example, =SUM(B2:B7) in the cell B9 will add up the values in B2, B3, B4, B5, B6 and B7 and display the result in B9. *Note*: the SUM function should only be used to add a continuous row or column of data.

The other function that you need to make sure you know how to use is the AVERAGE function. This is very similar to the SUM function in that it adds up all the values in the cells within the specified range. However, it then divides this result by the number of cells included in the range to give the mean average.

CHECK IT YOURSELF

The spreadsheet checklist on page 125 includes all the main calculation features you need to be able to use in your particular software. As you progress through the qualification, complete section 3 so that you can include this in your evidence folder as supplementary evidence.

Spreadsheet checklist

Section 1: layout

Page layout	Page size	☐
	Page orientation	☐
Page numbering	Positioning	☐
	Format	☐
Headers and footers	Date	☐
	Time	☐
	Filename	☐
Size	Columns	☐
	Rows	☐

Section 2: data formatting

Cell formats	Text	☐
	Numeric	
	integer	☐
	decimal	☐
	currency	☐
	Date	☐
Appearance	Different fonts	☐
	Size of text	☐
	Bold	☐
	Italics	☐
	Other	☐
Margins	Left and right	☐
	Top and bottom	☐
	Header and footer	☐

Section 3: calculations

Arithmetic calculations	Add	☐
	Subtract	☐
	Multiply	☐
	Divide	☐
Functions	Sum	☐
	Average	☐

Unit 205 Communicate Information Electronically

This unit contains three elements:

205.1 Transmit messages electronically
205.2 Receive messages electronically
205.3 Access and retrieve electronically stored information.

You need to demonstrate that you can identify and interpret correctly your customer's requirements. You will also need to show that you can work effectively with communications facilities to create and transmit electronically prepared information. This will include working with file attachments as required.

To meet the requirements of this unit, you should have a good basic understanding of the range of electronic information services and functions necessary to communicate electronically and the factors that will influence your choice to meet a specific requirement. You should understand the importance of accuracy and the checking facilities available within the software, the different output devices available and issues of confidentiality when producing this output.

What is information and communications technology (ICT)?

Information and communications technology is becoming accepted as the new term used to describe working with computers. We are no longer just concerned with the information and the technology to process it; the single most important aspect is to communicate this information. Speed, ever-reducing costs and general availability of communications technology, e-mail and the Internet have revolutionised the way we work and live.

Document transmission

Facsimile (fax)

The transmission of exact copies of documents across the telephone network has revolutionised many aspects of the way we work. This means of electronic communications has become a standard way of transmitting key documents. Any document, whether it is handwritten, contains pictures, diagrams, graphs, charts or typed text, can be transmitted at great speed for relatively low costs. More recently this facility has become a standard feature of computer-based electronic communications systems.

There are many benefits to most organisations in using faxes, including the following:

- Sending a fax is almost instant – you don't need to wait for the next day's mail or the messenger.
- The fax system is widely available – most organisations have at least one fax machine.
- The cost of sending a fax is relatively low compared with, for example, using a messenger.
- International standards have been set which means that you can send faxes to most parts of the world.
- A fax machine can be connected to any telephone socket, so it can be relocated very easily.
- The equipment is very compact and many models are portable.
- You can programme the machine to transmit a fax at a specified time, thus taking advantage of cheaper telephone rates.
- Most fax machines can receive documents automatically, so you don't have to be there when the document is received.
- Many computers have fax capabilities installed in them – you don't even need to print the document but can send the document from the screen or the file.

As with any communications system, good practice can ensure that everything runs smoothly:

- Include a front sheet – you need this to indicate details of whom the fax is from and the total number of pages so that the recipient can make sure it has all arrived safely.
- Check the quality of the original documents. Make sure the images are clear and the text is legible – if the original document is not black on white, is damaged or is on the wrong size of paper for the machine, it is a good idea to make a photocopy of the original and use the photocopy for the fax transmission.
- Leave a sufficient margin all around as the edges may distort.
- Damaged documents will not easily pass through the machine – make a photocopy and use that.
- Make sure you use the correct size of paper.
- Check the fax number before you send the message. The number dialled is usually shown in a display panel – make sure it is correct. If you are sending to a fax/phone number, you will need to make sure that it is set to receive faxes before you transmit, possibly by phoning the recipient to alert him or her to the incoming fax.

- Check received messages to ensure all the pages have transmitted and that they are legible. Call back immediately if the fax needs to be sent again.
- Faxes are usually fairly urgent, so make sure that incoming faxes are delivered speedily to the relevant person.

Faxes are transmitted using telephone lines. The cost of sending a fax is directly related to the length of time it takes to send it, the time of day when you send it and where you are sending it. If you send a fax of a document that has very little 'white space', that is, where most of the page has text or graphics on it, it will take longer for the fax to be transmitted and the cost will be greater.

For local transmissions, the costs are often far less than postage rates and, of course, the document will be received much more quickly. When you are sending documents long distances, the costs are greater than by post but you would weigh this against the time factor to decide what method is more appropriate. International faxing costs need to be considered in terms of costs compared with the time taken to use the postal system.

Although many organisations are now quite happy to receive orders, contracts, etc. by fax in order to speed up the process of dealing with the information, these copies are still largely unacceptable as legal documents. This means that once you have faxed the document you will also have to send the original by post or courier.

CHECK IT YOURSELF

Do you have access to a fax machine in your workplace? Is there a standard front page for all fax transmissions? How much, on average, does the transmission of a three-page fax cost? Is there a set of guidelines? Place a copy of them in your evidence folder. Enter this information in section 1 of the data communications checklist given on page 137.

Information transmission

Network communications

Many activities carried out on a day-to-day basis on a computer are only needed in the immediate work environment, but there are many reasons why the computer you work on may be part of a computer network.

Local area networks (LANs) exist where computers are located within relatively short distances of one another, usually within the same building. These are often used so that people within the organisation can share resources such as printers, high-capacity disk storage devices and software, and to enable a range of users to have access to the same data. An electronic mail system can also be established. Similar networks are also frequently set up using telecommunications systems, so that communication and sharing of resources can take place over a wider area (WANs). Many organisations also have links to external networks.

Electronic mail (e-mail)

Electronic mail, more commonly known as e-mail, is a communications system that enables you to send messages and information with the certainty that it has been placed in the recipient's mailbox. E-mail is a way of carrying out rapid, text-based communications both in and outside an organisation. In many organisations, the use of e-mail has replaced the memo and sometimes even letters.

To be able to use e-mail you need to have your computer connected to a network and have the appropriate e-mail software on the system. The e-mail system, like any other system within an organisation, has to be managed and supported. There will usually be a post-master who has responsibility for setting up each mailbox, maintaining mailing lists and other network-wide features.

E-mail can considerably improve the internal communications of an organisation, particularly if it is introduced with an appropriate training programme to ensure it is used effectively. However, like all communications systems, it is often used thoughtlessly.

When you are using e-mail you need to be aware of the following:

- E-mail is first read on a computer screen. If the message is too long, then it needs to be scrolled up and down, and this can make it much more difficult to take in the detail of the message. Short clear paragraphs are much easier to read on the screen.
- If you are using colours, think of the reader and remember that different screens are set to different levels of contrast and brightness and do not all have the same quality. What looks pleasing and exciting on your screen may not look quite the same to the recipient. It may be too bright, confusing and therefore difficult to read. Have you tried to read red writing on a purple background, for example?
- Read your message before you send it. Does it make sense? Have you missed out anything? We are not all proficient typists, so use the spell checker to help you correct those slips. You can usually set it up so that this is done automatically before you send the message. Once the 'send' command is pressed it is too late! You can't retrieve an e-mail unread, as you can a paper message.
- The written word needs to carry all the meaning you intend. There are no other clues, like tone of voice or facial expression, to assist. You need to take care when using capital letters, as they don't always convey the

right emphasis; capitals in an e-mail are considered to be the same as shouting! The tone is important. You will probably need to phrase messages to your boss in a different way from those sent to your peer group.

- How many e-mails do you print? E-mail should be reducing the paper flow, but does it increase yours?
- E-mail is only effective if all the users use it. How often do you read your mail?

E-mail not only lets you send and receive mail but also carry out a range of other functions:

- You can send a reply to any message you receive. As the name and e-mail address of the sender are already in the system, you only need to indicate the wish to send a reply and write it, and the system takes care of the rest.
- You can forward any message that you have received to any other person within the system.
- You can also attach documents and other computer files to your messages. This electronic exchange of files can significantly increase the usefulness of the system.
- Where you need to communicate with a group of people regularly, it is possible to set up a mailing list. Whenever you need to send them messages, you do not need to identify them individually but merely send your message using the mailing list.
- Mailboxes, just like any other mail system, need to be tidied up. You should delete messages that are no longer needed. Messages that need to be kept should be saved in folders, just as you would with a paper system.

E-mail systems operate readily not only across networks within the organisation but also across worldwide networks. Many organisations also provide external e-mail for their employees, usually as part of their links across the Internet. External e-mail has all the features of internal mail and can make a significant difference to business communications.

CHECK IT YOURSELF

What e-mail system do you have access to? Does it operate only within the organisation or are you able to send messages outside the organisation? Is there a post-master within the organisation who is responsible for maintaining the system? How frequently do you check e-mail messages during the working day? Enter this information in section 2 of the data communications checklist on page 137.

Electronic noticeboards

E-mail is a means of communicating directly and privately between individuals. However, quite a lot of communication in the workplace is intended for a wider audience. For this type of communication, there is a more effective system, known as electronic noticeboards or bulletin boards.

With this system, just one copy of the message is placed in a special mailbox which is accessible to all mail users. The message is managed by the person who placed it on the board, and he or she needs to delete it when it is no longer required. By using this system you ensure that no one is left off the mailing list, that only one copy exists within the system rather than one copy in each mailbox, and therefore that copies of the message do not need to be managed by every user.

CHECK IT YOURSELF

Do you have access to an electronic noticeboard? Enter this information in section 3 of the data communications checklist on page 137.

CHECK IT YOURSELF

Which method of communication would you use for the following tasks? Assume that the recipients will have access to fax and e-mail facilities. Put a ✔ in the box to indicate your choice. If you would follow up by post, put a ✔ in the 'post' box as well.

		Fax	E-mail	Post	Courier
1	A three-page document, of which you have only a printed copy, which needs to be with your customer by first thing next day	☐	☐	☐	☐
2	A highly confidential document that you have word processed and that has to be with your colleague based in another building by this afternoon at the latest	☐	☐	☐	☐
3	A short, urgent letter that you need to know has reached its destination	☐	☐	☐	☐
4	A word processed document with a great deal of scientific formulae. It				

	Fax	E-mail	Post	Courier
will need to be returned to you with suggested amendments by tomorrow	☐	☐	☐	☐
5 A poor-quality photocopy of a handwritten eight-page report that needs to be with a colleague at a different office within four days	☐	☐	☐	☐
6 A brief memo to be distributed to every head of department in the organisation	☐	☐	☐	☐
7 The agenda and notice of a planning meeting to be sent to a customer for a meeting scheduled for next Friday	☐	☐	☐	☐
8 Confirmation of an airline booking to be sent to the travel agents	☐	☐	☐	☐
9 A lease that contains plans and needs to be seen first by the client's solicitor and then signed by the client as soon as possible	☐	☐	☐	☐
10 Written details of a very urgent order you want your supplier to start processing this afternoon	☐	☐	☐	☐

External networks

Whatever kind of work you do and regardless of the type of organisation you work in, there is a need to communicate both inside and outside the organisation. The way that this is done is changing rapidly with the growth of worldwide networks and the ever-reducing costs of both the hardware and the communications software necessary to achieve this.

The Internet

The Internet has been around for a long time, but until fairly recently was primarily used by the US military Defense Advanced Research Projects Agency (DARPA) and the higher education sector Joint Academic NETwork (JANET). However, since the early 1990s its use has grown extremely rapidly both for home and business users. In very simple terms, it is a group of networks that use the same *protocol* (set of rules) to communicate.

To connect to the Internet you will usually have access via an Internet Provider (IP) and the system must be using the standard rules and procedures for connecting – TCP/IP (Transmission Control Protocol/Internet Protocol). If you are a home user or in a very small organisation you may be connecting via a modem, a device for converting analogue signals to digital signals and back again (modulator/demodulator). However, many businesses will be linking through a dedicated network line to the service provider.

There are various aspects of the Internet; the one that you are most likely to use is the World Wide Web (www). This is a graphical user interface (GUI) to access the resources on the Internet. What this means in simple terms is that it is 'user friendly' and works with pictures and interactive multimedia techniques. Using HTML (hypertext mark-up language), pages are linked to enable the user to 'surf the net'. By clicking on hyperlinks, the user is able to link to other pages all around the network. These links may lead to text, images, video clips, sounds and a wide range of services.

To be able to access the World Wide Web you need to have a browser. This is software that can read the HTML files. The web browser will enable you to navigate the web (move around the pages), to download images and text, and to print.

The information on the Internet is not organised, nor is it controlled or managed in any way. This means you need some assistance if you are to find what you are looking for. To be able to search effectively across this network of information you will often need to use one of the many *search engines* that are available. These are interactive services which have access to vast catalogues of hundreds of thousands of web sites which can be found through key word searches. There is an ever-increasing number of such tools available and some of the more sophisticated 'learn' about responses to searches so that they can improve their search results.

For many businesses, the primary use of the Internet is the provision of worldwide e-mail facilities. They have yet to appreciate the full capabilities or the impact that it may have on the way they conduct their business. For some, the Internet has the potential to provide opportunities for telling the rest of the world about their organisation and its products and services; it is becoming a powerful marketing medium. For other organisations it can provide, through the use of FTP (file transfer protocol), a means of transmitting data around the world.

CHECK IT YOURSELF

Do you have access to the Internet where you work? Find out the name of the provider and how the connection is made (dial-up or dedicated link).

What type of activities does the organisation use the Internet for? Is there a set of guidelines on using the Internet? Place a copy of them in your evidence folder. Enter this information in section 4 of the data communications checklist on page 137.

External databases

Many databases are available for reference purposes, and are not related to a specific area of business but can improve the efficiency of an organisation. The Internet can provide access to many of these, although access to some may be limited or restricted to subscribers or members of a closed group.

Not all remote databases are linked to the Internet, however. For many businesses, there are remote (external) databases which they need to access for their daily operations. The travel business needs access to airline bookings systems; for stock exchanges around the world, dealing takes place via access to online computerised databases; spare parts for cars are ordered through direct links to the manufacturers' databases. These are examples of *interactive* databases. Others are designed for reference only, such as Mediline.

Many of these uses are for closed user groups. The data is *not* available to the general public, nor is it free, but only available to paying subscribers. These types of links are usually connected using dial-up telephone links via a modem, dedicated telephone lines known as a megastream where the link is permanently established or, where the links need to be of particularly high speeds, Integrated Services Digital Network (ISDN) line.

CHECK IT YOURSELF

Do you have access to any external databases? How are they provided – through dial-up, megastream links or ISDN or some other connection? What type of information is available and what do you use it for? Enter this information in section 5 of the data communications checklist on page 137.

Videoconferencing

A relatively new and exciting development that could significantly change the way many people work is videoconferencing. One of the major concerns about the changing way of working, with an ever-increasing emphasis on the use of new technologies, is the reduction in opportunities for interaction between people.

Videoconferencing became popular during the Gulf war when many business people did not want to travel for fear of hijack or sabotage. It used to mean (and for some, still does) going to a special studio and using TV technology. Now, with videoconferencing equipment and communications links becoming more sophisticated, cheaper, and therefore more accessible, this is changing.

Each participant in a videoconference will need the following:

- a device to 'capture' video (a digital video camera);
- a microphone – although a conference can take place by 'talking' through the keyboard;
- speakers – assuming you are using voice contact;
- a computer – capable of handling the digitised video input;
- software to 'manage' the conference; and
- a communications channel – this could be ISDN or cable or across the Internet.

There are three ways that a conference can take place:

- Point-to-point – the simplest form of conference. One Internet user calls another. You need to know the Internet Provider's address of the other person.
- Group conference – a number of users simultaneously contact to a central computer which is running *reflector* software. You need to know the IP address of the reflector site.
- Broadcast conference – similar to a group conference, except the flow of communications is one way. The reflector site is used to transmit information to any connected user (see Figures 35, 36 and 37).

Figure 35 *Point-to-point conference*

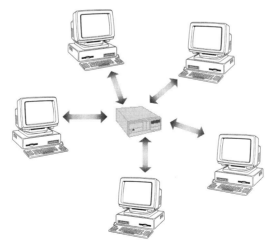

Figure 36 *Group conference*

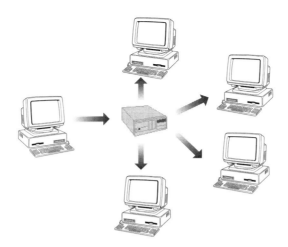

Figure 37 *Broadcast conference*

Data communications checklist

Section 1: fax	
Is there a standard front page?	Yes ☐ No ☐
What is the average cost of a three-page fax?	
Do you have a set of guidelines?	Yes ☐ No ☐
Section 2: e-mail	
Name of e-mail system	
Is this an internal *only* system?	Yes ☐ No ☐
If there is an external system, who is the provider?	
Who is the post-master?	
How frequently do you check your e-mail?	
Network software	
Version number	
Section 3: electronic communications	
Do you have electronic noticeboards?	Yes ☐ No ☐
Do you use an electronic diary or calendar?	Yes ☐ No ☐
Section 4: Internet	
Do you have access to the Internet?	Yes ☐ No ☐
Name of the Internet provider	
Method of connection	Dial-up ☐ Dedicated link ☐
What type of activities is it used for?	
Do you have a set of guidelines?	Yes ☐ No ☐
Section 5: external databases	
Do you have access to an external database?	Yes ☐ No ☐
How are connections made?	
What type of data is held?	
What do you use it for?	

Unit 207 Produce Documents Using Graphical Images

This unit contains three elements:

207.1 Identify and retrieve graphical images
207.2 Produce the required graphical images by manipulating image
207.3 Output the graphical images to the required destination.

You need to demonstrate that you can identify and correctly interpret your customer's requirements. You will also need to show that you can work effectively with graphics software to create, retrieve, edit, format and output graphical images within documents as required. This will include working with numerical data and applying relevant and appropriate graphical formats as required.

To meet the requirements of this unit, you should have a good basic understanding of the types of graphical images available and the range of graphic file formats used. You should also understand the features and functions necessary to produce and manipulate graphical images and the factors that will influence your choice to meet a specific requirement, the different input and output devices available and issues of security when producing this output.

Graphical images

There are two main types of graphical images: vectors and bitmaps.

Vector graphics are constructed using lines, and will typically be used for many technical applications as the resulting images are more precise and better able to be manipulated as objects. These are usually created using digitisers and graphics tablets, but can also be produced using programs to draw lines between Cartesian (x,y) co-ordinates.

There are specialist graphics packages for the drawing office, known as CAD (computer-aided design). With these, engineering drawings of all types can readily be produced (see Figure 38). Many of them can be used directly to control the manufacture of the designed item.

True three-dimensional images that can be rotated must be vector images. Computer games, where you move through a three-dimensional space and need to view objects from all directions, and virtual reality use this type of graphics.

Software that is used to produce an organisation chart, flow diagrams, etc. will also produce vector graphics (see Figure 39).

Bitmap images are created in pixels and consist of blocks of colour. Images that have been created through a scanning process will be in this form. Most painting and art packages produce images in this format (see Figure 40).

Company logos, pictures to be included in leaflets and graphical representations of data will usually have been created in this format. Depending on the quality of the graphics format and the package used, as they are increased in size, so the smoothness of the lines may be reduced.

Many drawing packages enable the artistic to produce high-quality images and to save these in digital form. There is also a vast range of 'clip art' which can be bought or is provided with software packages. Many popular images are available to enhance the presentation of documents. It is important to make sure, however, that when you are using images you have not created yourself, either from 'clip art' or by scanning them in, you are not breaking any copyright laws (see page 17).

Figure 38 *Cut-away drawing of the space shuttle* Columbia *produced using CAD software*

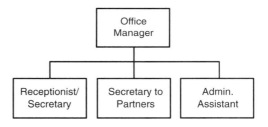

Figure 39 *Departmental organisation chart produced using charting software*

Figure 40 *Bitmap images can be (a) edited pixel by pixel and (b) produced using a paint package*

Business graphics

Most businesses need to produce facts and figures about how the business is doing in terms of its profitability and in comparison with previous years. They may also wish to compare their financial achievements with those of their competitors. While accountants and auditors might like to see this information presented as columns of numbers, most people find it much easier to understand the situation at a glance if the figures are displayed graphically.

Charts and graphs can be produced from business data using a variety of software including some word processing packages, most spreadsheet packages and a range of charting programs.

Graphical display of data

There are several different ways to display data graphically. Which one you use depends on the type of data, and the image that is most appropriate and visually effective for the particular purpose. It is often helpful to create a rough sketch of what you want to see in the graph before you create it.

Bar (column) charts

A bar chart is used to display graphically the *frequencies* of a set of data. It is drawn with either horizontal or vertical bars of comparative lengths.

Bar charts are particularly suitable if you want to compare different quantities over a period of time, or to display clearly the different amounts for a range of items.

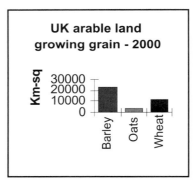

Figure 41 *Vertical bar chart*

An example of a vertical bar chart is given in Figure 41 and shows how many (frequency) square kilometres of arable land in the UK were used for growing barley, oats and wheat in 1999.

An example of a horizontal bar chart is given in Figure 42 and compares the value (frequency) in thousands of pounds of electrical equipment sales in the financial year 1999–2000.

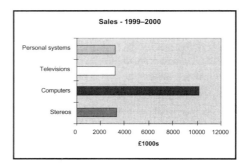

Figure 42 *Horizontal bar chart*

Pie charts

Sometimes you may wish to display the relative frequencies of the data. This is done by calculating the frequencies as a share of the whole, most often by using percentages of the whole (each item's frequency divided by the total and multiplied by 100). Each frequency is represented as a portion of the whole 'pie', that is, as a percentage of 360 degrees of a circle.

This type of chart requires relatively complex calculations and is not easy to draw when using a pen and paper, but when using a computer all the hard work is done for you by the software!

Figure 43 displays the data used for the bar chart in Figure 41 but showing each data item (barley, oats and wheat) as a percentage of the total land use.

Figure 44 shows the value of sales of electrical goods in the financial year 1999–2000 (see Figure 42) as percentages of the total sales of the organisation. The labels for the segments have been included in a legend.

Line graphs

When you want to show a *trend* in your data, it is often best to use a line graph. This shows a number of points joined together by a line. Each data value is plotted and then joined by a line which shows the change visually.

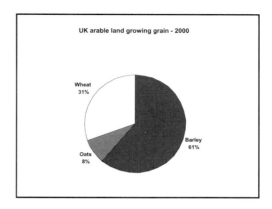

Figure 43 *Pie chart of the data shown in Figure 41*

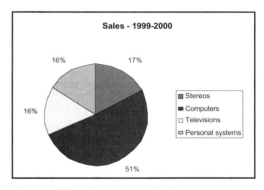

Figure 44 *The chart of the data shown in Figure 42*

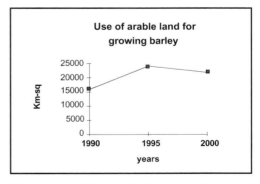

Figure 45 *Line graph showing a single trend*

An example of the data for arable land used for the production of barley in the three years 1990, 1995 and 2000 is best represented in a line graph (see Figure 45).

Line graphs can be particularly effective when a number of trends are displayed on the same graph. Figure 46 shows the trends in the sales of each of the four categories of electrical goods over a period of three years. If you were a business manager, this graph could help you decide which product you might want to concentrate on, and which you might consider discontinuing.

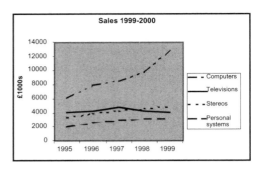

Figure 46 *Line graph showing multiple trends*

CHECK IT YOURSELF

When displaying business data graphically, it is important that you use the most appropriate and effective type of chart. You will need to consider the content of the data, the purpose of the chart and by whom the chart is going to be used. For example, the accountant will want to be able to see the exact values for the company's turnover, whilst shareholders may be more concerned with seeing at a glance the extent of the increase on last year's figures.

Which type of chart would you use for each of the following tasks? Put a ✔ in the box to indicate your choice.

	Bar chart	Pie chart	Line graph
1 The value of sales each month in the region in the past six months, for use at a meeting of sales managers	☐	☐	☐
2 Actual profit earned from items in the company's range of products, to be included in the financial director's report to shareholders	☐	☐	☐
3 The makeup of the workforce by age (five ranges) for the Annual Report	☐	☐	☐

	Bar chart	Pie chart	Line graph
4 The proportion of production costs accounted for by labour, materials, plant, power and distribution	☐	☐	☐
5 Income generated this year by each department in a firm of solicitors	☐	☐	☐
6 A comparison of monthly expenditure against budgets during the first three months of the financial year	☐	☐	☐
7 Fluctuations in the rate of exchange of the pound against the US dollar over the past four years	☐	☐	☐
8 The percentage of staff employed in each department	☐	☐	☐

Producing and manipulating images

To be an 'expert user' of graphics creation software you will need a wide range of techniques and skills. All full-feature software will enable you to produce highly complex and well-presented images.

When using most drawing software, there will be a number of predefined shapes that you can use; these will include rectangles, circles and lines. You will also be able to select the type and weight (thickness) of line and can include arrow heads at one, or both, ends of the line. There will also be a 'free-hand' drawing tool for the more expert or artistic.

When working with graphical images, colour and patterns are often very important. You will have a wide variety of colours available to choose from both for the outlines that you draw and to fill the shapes you have created; you may also be able to 'mix' your own colours. When deciding how best to use these facilities, you will need to take into account what form the final output will take. Will the final document be paper-based or projected on a screen? Do you have a high-quality colour printer, or will the document then be photocopied and be better presented using fill patterns?

Many of the images that you will need to use may already exist. They will often be a paper-based version that needs to be turned into a digital image. You will need to use a scanner with appropriate image-capture and manipulation software to do this. Using a scanner is now a relatively straightforward process, but you definitely improve with practice! Spending a little extra time ensuring that the image is right at this stage will save you time later when you are producing the final document.

As the digital storage of images has progressed, a considerable number of different ways of storing the images has been developed. You need to be aware of the more common ones, when they are most likely to be used and which ones the software you use is capable of handling.

CHECK IT YOURSELF

Which of the images below can your software process? Tick the relevant boxes.

Image	File extension	✔
graphics interchange format	gif	
tag image file format	tif	
windows meta file	wmf	
targa	tga	
windows bitmap	bmp	
windows paintbrush	pcx	
encapsulated postscript	eps	
JPEG	jpg	
drawing exchange file	dxf	
photo cd	pcd	

Graphics are rarely the only part of a document and are more usually included to improve the overall presentation. This means that when you are working with images you need to be able to insert and manipulate them to fit with the overall design of the document. You should be able to position the image exactly where it is required and understand the importance of how to change the size of the image without distorting it; that is, maintaining the *aspect ratio*.

The electronic storage of images will often require considerable storage capacity. You will need to ensure that the medium you use is appropriate – a floppy disk can store only 1.44Mb of data so a complex document with a number of images may be too large to fit on one. There are a number of software utilities available so that you can compress the data to fit on to a disk. You should make sure that you are aware of what is available in your organisation and how to use them.

Whether you are producing documents using graphics software, word processing software or any other package which results in paper-based output, many of the presentation considerations are the same. You will need to make sure that you are fully aware of the standards and conventions required by your organisation (see 'House styles' in Unit 202 on page 101).

Many of the layout features are the same; you will need to know how to change the orientation of the page, include headers and footers and adjust the four margins of the page (top, bottom, left and right). You will need to know how to use features such as page numbering and date/time stamping and to achieve 'best fit' for your data.

When considering output involving images, a major factor must be quality. You should make sure that you know how to adjust the parameters in the printer setup to ensure the best results. A major factor in deciding quality is measured in dpi (dots per inch) – you should be printing with a minimum of 600 dpi for high-quality output. If you are printing in black and white, you may need to be using greyscale so that the quality of image is high. The best way to find out what works best for your equipment and software is to experiment. Change one aspect of the print properties and see whether this improves the overall product, but make sure you only change one parameter at a time and that you keep a record for future use.

You will also need to know how to use specialist stationery, and in particular transparencies. It is extremely important that the correct type of medium is used – there are different ones for laser and ink-jet printers and others that are not suitable at all. If you use the wrong ones, they are likely to melt inside the printer and may completely destroy the printer mechanisms.

CHECK IT YOURSELF

The graphical images checklist on page 146 includes all the main features that you need to be able to use in your particular software. As you progress towards your qualification, complete this checklist and include it in your evidence folder as supplementary evidence.

Graphical images checklist

Section 1: image creation		
Image types	Bitmap (new)	☐
	Bitmap (amend)	☐
	Vector (new)	☐
	Vector (amend)	☐
Input devices	Keyboard	☐
	Mouse	☐
	Scanner	☐
	Digitiser	☐
	Other	☐
Output	Greyscale	☐
	Colour	☐
	Transparencies	☐
	Other	☐
Section 2: image attributes		
Colour	Predefined	☐
	Define own	☐
	Effects	☐
Patterns	Predefined	☐
	Define own	☐
Form	Size	☐
	Shape	☐
Section 3: image presentation		
Layout	Size	☐
	Orientation	☐
Manipulation	Rotation	☐
	Scaling	☐
	Inversion	☐

Graphical images checklist (continued)

Section 4: elements		
Line	Type	☐
	Thickness	☐
Shape	Predefined	☐
	Define own	☐
	Objects	☐
Text	Different fonts	☐
	Size of text	☐
	Bold	☐
	Italics	☐

Unit 212 Maintain and Use Databases

This unit contains three elements:

212.1 Retrieve and enter data to update databases
212.2 Extract the required information
212.3 Output specified information to the required destination.

You need to demonstrate that you can identify and correctly interpret your customer's requirements. You will also need to show that you can work effectively with database software to retrieve, edit, manipulate and output data using existing single-table database files as required. This will include working with text and numeric data and applying relevant and appropriate queries and sorts as required.

To meet the requirements of this unit, you should have a good basic understanding of the structure of single-table databases and the range of database features and functions necessary to maintain and manipulate database files and the factors that will influence your choice to meet a specific requirement. You should understand the importance of accuracy and the checking facilities available within the software and the requirements of the data protection legislation, the different output devices available and issues of confidentiality when producing this output.

What is a database?

A database is an organised collection of related data that is defined and accessed by a set of programs known as a database management system (DBMS).

Each item of data, for example a name, is held in a *field*. The collection of related data fields are treated as a unit and are known as a *record*. The complete set of data records is held in a data *file* or *table* (see Figure 47).

Most of the time when you use a database you want to work with only selected parts of the complete file. To do this you need to know how the database has been structured.

Each field is defined when the database is set up. For each field the following information needs to be given:

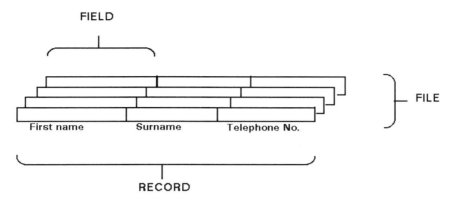

Figure 47 *A data file or table*

- field name - this is how you refer to the field;
- data type - this indicates the type of data that can be held, text or number;
- field size - this defines the maximum number of characters allowed in the field (not used for numeric data); and
- format - this indicates how the data is to be displayed, e.g. the number of decimal places for a numeric field.

Working with a simple database

Many people keep simple, paper-based databases to assist with their work. This often takes the form of a card-index file or pages in a lever-arch file. How would you set up a simple filing system to keep the names, addresses, telephone numbers, etc. for the staff in a large organisation or department? You might decide to have a record card for each person. The card could be divided up with spaces for the different items, the fields, of data needed, and so might look like the record card in Figure 48.

Name:			
Address:			
City:		Post Code:	
Telephone No:		Fax No:	
e-mail:			
Job Title:			
Department:			

Figure 48 *A record card*

These cards would be organised in a box file, probably in alphabetical order of name with a divider card for each initial letter. It would then be a very quick and simple process if you wanted to find the details of an individual, as long as you knew his or her name.

However, if you needed to find all the telephone numbers of the staff in a particular department, you would need to go through, card by card, checking the department and extracting the names and telephone numbers and then write out or word process a list with this information. This would be a very slow and time-consuming activity.

A simple, single-table database will do all this for you, and quite a lot more.

You would need to define each of the fields on your record card, identifying an appropriate name, the data type and the field size and, where necessary, the format. This is one of the most important stages in setting up the database. You must make sure that you have defined all the fields that you need, that they are able to hold the data in the way that you need it, and that you have allowed sufficient but not excessive space to store the data (see Figure 49).

Field name	Data type	Field size	Format	Comments
Surname	Text	20	Initial capital	This should be held separately from the first name so that you can carry out a true alphabetic sort
First Name	Text	15	Initial capital	
Address	Text	35		This might be divided into two or three separate fields so that the data could also be used for mailing labels
City	Text	15	Initial capital	
Post Code	Text	14	Upper case letters and numbers	
Telephone No.	Text	15	Numbers and spaces only	This is *not* a numeric field – telephone numbers are not real numbers but codes that happen to consist of numbers
Fax No.	Text	15	Numbers and spaces only	Same as telephone number
e-mail	Text	25	No spaces	
Job Title	Text	25		
Department	Text	1	One letter	It is quite common to use some kind of code to shorten the department's name and to ensure consistency, e.g. S = Sales F = Finance P = Production C = Customer Care

Figure 49 *Fields for a single-table database*

One of the most important aspects of working with a database is ensuring the integrity of the data (see page 5). The first stage in ensuring the integrity is at the point of input. Most database packages have a wide range of facilities and features to assist and support you in this. Although each database package will be organised in a particular way, there will be a number of standard facilities available.

The core of the database software is there to assist you in defining the structure of the data files. Although it is then possible to enter data directly into this file, the presentation and validation techniques using this method are very limited.

To improve the quality of the input screens, you will usually be able to design on-screen forms; these can be laid out to suit your needs and, with appropriate use of colours, fonts and images, can reflect the organisation's house style. These will also be able to assist in controlling the quality of the input, e.g. you may be able to have 'pick-lists' to choose the data from, check boxes to select an option, and dates can be validated to make sure they are real dates. If the data is going to be input from a paper document it is usually a good idea to try to make the screen look like the form; that way fewer mistakes are likely to be made.

In your simple staff information database, you could have a 'pick-list' for the department codes. This could be set up so that the list you choose from gives both the code and what it stands for. You could still choose the wrong department but you couldn't put in a code that did not represent any department (see Figure 50).

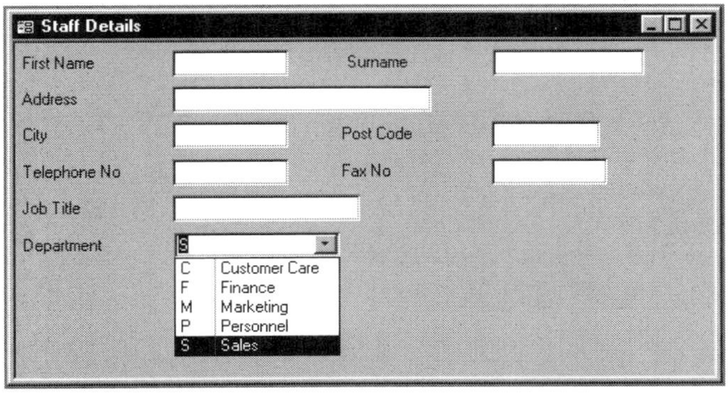

Figure 50 *Input screen showing 'pick-list'*

Manipulating data

Once accurate data is in the database, the key to successful use of that data is a good understanding of how to manipulate it to meet your needs. As you will need to make enquiries on the data, there will be some form of query language available. In many database packages this will be a simple query-by-example (QBE) screen that you fill in to specify the fields and the criteria for the selection required. This screen will also let you sort the data on one or more fields.

You would, for example, be able to select all the staff in a particular department and display their names in alphabetical order. To do this you should specify which fields you want. You should also specify the selection criteria. This may look something like this:

Department = 'S' (to select all the records for the sales department)

You would also need to specify which field or fields you wished to use to sort the data and whether this was in ascending (A to Z; 1 to 100) or descending (Z to A; 100 to 1) order. As you want this list in alphabetical order of name you should specify Surname followed by FirstName and in ascending order (see Figure 51).

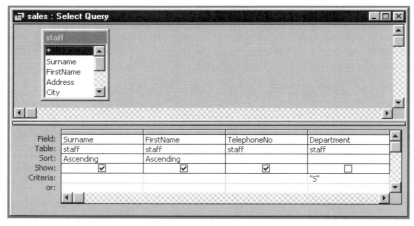

Figure 51 *A QBE screen in Microsoft Access*

CHECK IT YOURSELF

The database checklist on page 155 includes all the main data manipulation features you need to be able to use in your particular software. As you progress through the qualification, complete section 2 so that you can include this in your evidence folder as supplementary evidence.

To improve the quality of the presentation, you could set up an 'on-screen' form designed to display your results.

Alternatively, you may wish to print out the results of this selection so that you can refer to it whenever you need to. To do this you will need to produce a database report. In your database package you will have a facility to do this; it is called a report generator. This will let you define the fields to be printed and the order in which they are to be displayed. It will also, as with any paper-based output, let you specify any headers and footers. Database reports are, however, slightly different in their structure from most other paper-based documents in that there can be several different headers and footers (see Figure 52).

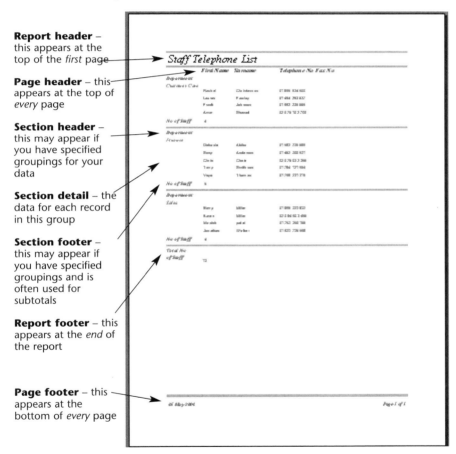

Report header –
this appears at the top of the *first* page

Page header – this appears at the top of *every* page

Section header –
this may appear if you have specified groupings for your data

Section detail – the data for each record in this group

Section footer –
this may appear if you have specified groupings and is often used for subtotals

Report footer – this appears at the *end* of the report

Page footer – this appears at the bottom of *every* page

Figure 52 *Headers and footers in database reports*

Whether you are producing documents using database software, word processing software or any other package which results in paper-based output, many of the presentation considerations are the same. You will need to make sure that you are fully aware of the standards and conventions required by your organisation (see 'House styles' in Unit 202 on page 101).

Many of the layout features are the same; you will need to know how to change the orientation of the page, include headers and footers and adjust the four margins of the page (top, bottom, left and right). You should know how to use features such as page numbering and date/time stamping and to achieve 'best fit' for your data.

CHECK IT YOURSELF

The database checklist on page 155 includes all the main layout features you need to be able to use in your particular software. As you progress through the qualification, complete section 3 so that you can include this in your evidence folder as supplementary evidence.

Database checklist

Section 1: data structures		
Data types	Text	☐
	Numeric	☐
Data characteristics	Name	☐
	Type	☐
	Size	☐
Formats	Numeric	☐
	integer	☐
	decimal	☐
	currency	☐
	Text	☐
Section 2: data manipulation		
Simple queries	Selected records	☐
	Selected fields	☐
	Multiple – AND	☐
Sort	Order	☐
	ascending	☐
	descending	☐
	Single field	☐
	Multiple fields	☐
Section 3: layout		
Page layout	Page size	☐
	Page orientation	☐
Page numbering	Positioning	☐
	Format	☐
Headers and footers	Date	☐
	Time	☐
	Filename	☐
	Sections	☐

Appendix Applying for a Job

There are a number of different ways to apply for a job. You might reply to an advertisement or could be making an enquiry on the recommendation of a friend. You might register with an employment agency which will try to find you a job or you might even try 'cold selling', that is, approaching employers directly to see if they have any vacancies for which they might consider you. If you have access to the Internet you might even try applying for a job using the latest technology.

Employers have different requirements when they are recruiting staff. Some will want you to write a letter of application, some will have an application form that you must complete and others will ask you to give them a copy of your CV. Many will also want you to submit some sort of statement about why you are particularly suitable for the job.

This whole process of job applications can be quite stressful and time consuming. What you can do to reduce some of the pressures is to prepare outline documents with all the main details collated in a coherent form. All you will then need to do is update them, if necessary, and customise them for each specific job application.

What is a CV?

CV stands for curriculum vitae. It is the main document you can use to describe yourself to a prospective employer. It contains details about your personal background, your aspirations and ambitions, your work experience, your skills and knowledge, your education and other relevant activities.

Your CV is not something that you can create once – it needs to be kept up to date. It therefore makes sense to set it up as a word processed document that you can amend whenever you need to. With the high level of word processing skills that you will have developed while working towards your qualification, you should be able to produce a professional and well-presented document. This will not only enable you to describe yourself but will also give you the opportunity to demonstrate your IT and presentation skills to any prospective employer.

The layout and content of your CV will need to be varied according to its purpose. You will usually find that you will need to amend its emphasis to meet the specific requirements of the job you are applying for. It will need to be different if it is submitted as the main document, together with a letter of application, rather than accompanying an application form. It is also useful to have an outline CV which just contains the basic facts – dates, addresses, etc. – so that you can refer to it when completing any forms.

CV layout

As with most business documents, the style and presentation of CVs have changed over the years. This has to some extent been influenced by the technology available to produce the final document.

You need to be mindful of the audience for whom your CV is written. As this is a document that you want to be read in full, it must not be too long. It needs to have a clear presentation and be organised so that the reader can quickly gain an impression of you, your knowledge, expertise and skills. It is usual to organise your CV into distinct sections, making it easy to find the required information. Your CV needs to include sections on personal details, work experience, relevant skills and expertise, education and training, interests and hobbies, etc. and references. As an introduction, you could include a brief summary or profile of yourself, highlighting your most relevant achievements and skills. You might also include a section describing your personal objectives, giving details of your aspirations and goals.

Personal details need to include:

- Name – if you have changed your name you might need to indicate this, particularly if some of your qualification are in a different name or referees know you by another name.
- Title – you might want to include this, especially if you wish to be addressed in a particular way such as Ms rather than Mrs or Miss, or Dr, etc.
- Date of birth – many prospective employers will want this information.
- Address – obviously, a prospective employer needs to have an address, and possibly also a telephone number and even an e-mail address, at which to contact you.

There may be additional basic information that you wish to include here such as National Insurance number, work permit details, etc.

CHECK IT YOURSELF

Complete section 1 of the CV information sheet on page 164 with all your personal details.

Work experience is the section that provides details of each organisation for which you have worked. It should be presented in chronological order. You should include the name and address of the organisation, the dates you were working there, the title of the job you held, a brief description of the post specifying its tasks and responsibilities, and the salary or wages you received. If you are looking for your first job it is particularly important to include any work experience placements you have been on, any holiday or weekend jobs and any voluntary work you might have done.

CHECK IT YOURSELF

Complete section 2 of the CV information sheet on page 164 with details of your work experience.

Relevant skills and knowledge is the section where you can identify the skills and expertise you have that are particularly relevant to the type of work you are seeking. You need to emphasise the IT skills you have, specifying which software packages you can use and indicating some of the ways in which you have used them.

CHECK IT YOURSELF

Complete section 3 of the CV information sheet on page 165 with details of the skills and knowledge you have that would be of interest to a prospective employer.

Education and training needs to give information about your education from age 11. This should include each school, college or other organisation you attended in chronological order. You should give the name and address of the institution, the dates you attended, the subjects studied and qualifications gained. If you attended part time, you should also indicate this. As well as formal education, you should include any training courses you have attended which are particularly relevant to the type of work that you are seeking, or which may increase your employability, e.g. a first aid certificate.

CHECK IT YOURSELF

Complete section 4 of the CV information sheet on page 165 with details of your education and training and any training courses you have attended.

Interests and hobbies. Most employers are interested to know a little about their prospective employees in terms of what they do outside work. This is where your personality can come across in your CV. Prospective employers will be particularly interested in any activities that show leadership skills (e.g. leading Scout or Guide activities), teamwork (e.g. member of a sports team) or ones that involve accepting responsibilities (e.g. acting as a treasurer for a club or society).

CHECK IT YOURSELF

Complete section 5 of the CV information sheet on page 165 with information about your interests, hobbies and activities outside work.

References. Prospective employers will usually want to contact at least two people who can confirm your suitability for employment. They will want the name and relationship to you (e.g. manager, tutor) of people who can provide information about your attitude to work, your enthusiasm, commitment and skills. They will want to know that you are a reliable, honest and punctual worker. They will also need to be able to confirm your experience, qualifications and knowledge. For some jobs they will be particularly interested in confirming aspects that relate specifically to the type of job. For example, if the job involves working with the public, they will be interested in your ability to work with and relate to people, or if you are going to be handling money they will wish to ensure that you are trustworthy. Remember to ask permission from any one you wish to use as a referee *before* giving details to a prospective employer.

CHECK IT YOURSELF

Complete section 6 of the CV information sheet on page 165 with details of two people you could ask to act as your referees.

You should also include a *personal objectives* section in your CV, in which you can show that this is the area of work or job for you. You will need to include a statement about how you wish your career to develop, and ensure that this relates to the opportunities in the job you are applying for.

What are your job/career plans? What sort of job are you looking for now, and what sort of work would you like to be doing in five years' time? Write a few clear sentences about both your short- and long-term goals. Make sure they are realistic and that they make use of the skills, experience and knowledge gained in this NVQ. At this stage, as you are not applying for a particular job, this will probably be a fairly general statement, but remember that it will need to be revised each time you use it to reflect the particular job application.

Although you should place the *summary* or *profile* near the beginning of your CV, you can only write it when you have compiled all the details about yourself. This summary will be some of the first information that a prospective employer will read about you. It will therefore need to give them information that will make them want to read the rest of your CV.

What are the most important pieces of information about you that a prospective employer wants to know? What are you best at (include both your vocational expertise and your interpersonal skills)? What have been your greatest work-related achievements? Write a few brief, concise sentences to describe yourself. You may wish to include your achievements as bullet points. As with all the sections of your CV, remember that it will need to be revised each time you use it to reflect the particular job application.

It is important to make sure that your CV accounts for all the time from your secondary education onwards. If you had some time out after school before going to college or embarking on your career (e.g. a gap year), indicate this and say what you were doing, whether travelling, gaining skills or doing voluntary work, etc. If you have had time out as a carer (e.g. of children or sick/elderly relatives), include this information.

If you have access to the Internet, there are several web sites that provide information on how to create a CV. Some of these offer a range of CV writing services which you would have to pay for, but others give free advice and guidance on how to create your own.

An example of a CV is given on page 162.

Application forms

The questions in application forms can vary quite considerably. Many organisations will require you to complete a form. In addition, they may specifically state that you should *not* include a CV, or that a CV may be included but the form must still be completed in full. Much of the form will ask for basic details about yourself, your previous work experience and education and qualifications you have gained. If you have prepared an outline CV, most of this is simply a matter of transferring the information to the form. There will also be a section (often little more than a blank page) where you are asked to write about why and how you are particularly suitable for the job. This is almost always the most important part of the form, and where you need to concentrate your efforts. In this section you should include information from your CV such as the summary, personal objectives, skills and knowledge, and relevant experience.

Make sure that you first read any guidance about how the form is to be completed. It may specify that the form must be filled in with black ink – this is usually to ensure that good-quality photocopies can be made – or it may require that it is hand written. Some employers engage specialists to analyse your handwriting!

If you are applying electronically for a job, you may be asked to complete an electronic application form. This will be very similar to filling in a paper-based form, but be careful – if you are completing a form online, you should check it very thoroughly on screen before you send it; once the send or OK button is pressed it has been sent and cannot be stopped!

Letter of application

A letter of application will usually be used where there is no application form. Its purpose is to introduce your CV and to make clear which job you are applying for. You need to state clearly where you heard about the job and then highlight the particular skills and experience that you have which make you suitable for the position. It is often appropriate to identify some recent training or work experience which is particularly relevant. You should also include details about your availability for interview and when you would be able to start work should a post be offered to you. Don't make the letter more than one page long – it needs to be clear, brief and very much to the point. An example of a letter of application is given on page 163.

When making an application in this way, you will need to ensure that your CV is comprehensive and supplies sufficient detail about yourself and why you should be considered for the job in question.

Curriculum Vitae

Personal Details

Name:	Dianne Porter
Date of birth:	8 August 1977
Address:	12a Wiley Street
	Birmingham B23 XX2
Telephone:	01234 567 8901
E-mail:	dianne@abc.def.uk
NI Number:	HT 12 34 56 G

Profile

An efficient administrator with experience in the hotel industry and voluntary sector. Wide range of current IT skills recently applied in an electric office environment. Able to work on own initiative and as part of a team. Always keen to acquire and apply new skills.

Work Experience

Waverley Hotel **Oct 1994–May 1996** **Receptionist**
Duties included receiving and registering guests, dealing with booking enquiries, making up guests' bills and some associated general clerical tasks.

The Red Lion Hotel **June 1996–April 1998** **Hotel administrator**
Responsible for ensuring that all clerical and administration tasks were up to date. This included computerised guest booking system, use of spreadsheet for basic accounting and word processing general correspondence.

Wiley Play Group **January 1999 onwards** **Volunteer helper**
Help with range of activities for children, both indoors and outside. Assist with the general clerical activities, including the word processing of letters for parents and producing information leaflets and posters.

Relevant Skills and Knowledge

I have good general IT skills and have recent experience using the following packages:

Word processing:	Word 2000
	WordPerfect 6
Spreadsheet:	Excel 2000
Presentation:	Powerpoint 2000

Education and Training

Hillside School	Sept 1988–July 1994	5 GCSEs, including Maths and English Typewriting Processing Stage 1
FE College (evening class)	Sept 1997–July 1998	Computer Literacy Certificate
FE College (part time)	Oct 1999–July 2000	NVQ Level 2 Using IT

Interests and Hobbies

I am a keen gardener and also enjoy rock climbing. I have a two-year-old daughter for whom I have been the primary carer since May 1998, but who starts full time at nursery in August.

Personal Objectives

I have recently updated my IT skills and would now like to have the opportunity to use them in an office environment, possibly also using the interpersonal skills I acquired whilst working in the hotel industry. I enjoy assisting others in the use of the technology and would be interested in working in a job where I also had a user support and training role.

Michelle Walters
Head of Youth Services Team
Council Chambers
Hemel Hempstead
Herts
HP 1 4JD

15 June 2000

Dear Ms Walters

Office Administrator

I am writing in response to the advertisement for the above position in the local newspaper last Thursday. Please find enclosed a copy of my CV, which includes details of two referees whom you may contact to confirm my suitability for the post.

Currently, I am completing a course at the local college in the use of a wide range of IT office applications, including word processing, spreadsheets, databases and the use of electronic communication systems. When I complete the course at the beginning of July, I will have gained an NVQ Level 2 award in Using Information Technology and will be looking to return to full-time work.

I have recently been working on a voluntary basis for a national charity in their local offices. During this time I have gained considerable experience in the application of the skills acquired in my studies. I am an extremely conscientious and enthusiastic person and like to work with others as part of a team.

I have also enclosed a stamped, addressed envelope for your reply.

I look forward to hearing from you.

Yours sincerely

CV information sheet

Section 1: personal details	
Name – including title	
Date of birth	
Address	
Telephone number, e-mail address, etc.	
NI number, etc.	
Section 2: work experience	
Employer (1) details	
Start and end date	
Job title	
Salary	
Description	
Employer (2) details	
Start and end date	
Job title	
Salary	
Description	
Employer (3) details	
Start and end date	
Job title	
Salary	
Description	

CV information sheet (continued)

Section 3: relevant skills and knowledge

Section 4: education and training

School (from age 11) name
and address

Start and end dates

Qualifications

College name and address

Start and end dates

Qualifications

Other courses attended

Section 5: interests and hobbies

Section 6: references

Referees – name, job title
and address
(1)

(2)

Example job advertisements

Corporate/Banking Law PAs
£25,000 + benefits

Due to continued expansion, we are seeking high calibre Corporate/Banking Law PAs to work in our new London offices. The workload is high and there will always be a need for overtime but the atmosphere in the office is extremely friendly, making your working day an enjoyable one.

An excellent knowledge of the major software packages including Word 97/2000, Excel and PowerPoint is required, along with a professional telephone manner, an eye for detail and good organisational skills.

Please send a covering letter and copy of your CV to:

Nita Bokil, Personnel Officer, Hodges and Scott, 5 Tower Centre, London, EC2 2LS

IT TRAINING
We are a large, lively firm of solicitors.
We are looking for a bright and enthusiastic person to join our IT team to cross-train users from WordPerfect to Word 2000. Further training needs may include Lotus Notes and other Windows applications. Candidates should have a thorough knowledge of Word and other computer applications with some experience of training and an understanding of secretarial work. This is a challenging post which offers an attractive salary package and opportunity for development to the right applicant.

Please send your cv to:
Mrs S Laundy
Ross and Son
10 Broad Street
Nottingham
NG1 2LS

Team Secretary
£25,000pa + benefits

Job Description:
The role involves working in the marketing department for a small team of four. Updating the customer database and producing presentations are the main responsibilities of the role.
Skills Required:
Excellent computer skills are essential. A good working knowledge of Microsoft Word 97/2000, Access and PowerPoint is needed. The role requires someone with a really proactive manner, with a willingness to learn about the industry. Proven experience of databases is desirable, although full training will be given. An excellent eye for detail and the ability to work in a relatively pressured environment are essential.
For further details please contact us:
Oakleaf Recruitment
21 High Street
Basingstoke
Hants
RG21 2SY

Tel: 01256 623411

OFFICE ADMINISTRATOR
HEMEL HEMPSTEAD
£9.00 p.h.

Experienced Office Administrator required to manage a busy Youth Service office. Enthusiastic person with ability to work on own and carry out office tasks is needed to complete the team.

Essential: Word processing, organised
Desirable: Spreadsheet and E-mail

Send your CV and letter of application to: Michelle Walters, Head of Youth Services Team, Council Chambers. Hemel Hempstead, Herts, HP1 4JD

PA to Campaigns Director
£15,250 – £16,735 (depending on experience)

Excellent opportunity to work in a lively, expanding charitable organisation. Reporting to the Campaigns Director, you will be responsible for dealing with day-to-day correspondence, producing reports and overseeing the running of the office.

You must be an enthusiastic team player, with the ability to work on your own initiative and to cope with a number of tasks at any one time. You will also need a high level of computer proficiency in the major software packages including MS Word, Excel and PowerPoint. A knowledge of MS Access is desirable, however full training will be given. You should have at least 3 years' secretarial experience.

If you would like to be considered for this position, please send a covering letter outlining the qualities you can bring to the organisation along with a copy of your CV to:

Mr L Leblanc
Campaigns Director
Global Aid
Africa House
Glasgow
G4 5SJ

NVQ Glossary

Assessors Persons responsible within the NVQ centre for checking the quality of the evidence (work) produced by the candidates and for making sure it covers all the requirements of the set of standards.

Awarding body The organisation, approved by the QCA, which awards the qualification (e.g. OCR Examinations Board).

Competence Ability to carry out the activities specified by the performance criteria to a particular standard.

Element Each unit consists of a number of elements. Candidates need to demonstrate competence in all elements of a unit to be awarded the unit.

Element knowledge The knowledge and understanding necessary to be able to carry out the work-based activities.

Evidence The products, statements and other records that demonstrate competence. Organised into a portfolio and assessed against the standards.

External verifier Person appointed by the awarding body to ensure the NVQ centre is carrying out the assessment to the required national standards.

Internal verifier The person within the NVQ centre with responsibility for ensuring that all the assessment in the centre is consistent and is being carried out to national standards. The link person with the awarding body's external verifier.

ITNTO Information Technology National Training Organisation – the computer industry lead body which sets the occupational standards.

NVQ National Vocational Qualification – a standard that has been introduced throughout England and Wales specifically for work-based qualifications.

Performance criteria The things a candidate must be able to do satisfactorily in order to be able to claim the award.

QCA Qualifications and Curriculum Authority – the organisation that oversees the standards and approves the qualifications set by the awarding bodies.

Range statements Set out the situations and conditions in which the candidates must be able to work and the equipment they must be able to use.

Standards The set of units defined by the industry lead body that describes the knowledge, skills and level of competence required for the area of work.

Unit All NVQs consist of a number of units. A unit is a complete section of knowledge and is the smallest award possible. Most NVQs consist of a number of mandatory units and some optional units.

IT Glossary

Alternate (ALT) key   A key, similar to the control key, that is used together with another key to send a modified code to the computer.

Archive   An archive copy of a file is made when you no longer need the file in the main working environment but need to keep a copy for reference or possible use in the future.

Backup   An operating utility which lets you make a security copy of your files – this is not a directly usable copy but can be restored if required.

Bitmap graphics   Images created in pixels, i.e. consist of blocks of colour.

Byte   The unit of measurement for counting the size of various parts of a computer – generally speaking the computer space necessary to hold one character or code.

CD   Optical disk which is capable of holding high volumes of data – it can only be created once and is therefore not appropriate for data that needs to change.

CD-ROM   Compact disk – read-only memory drive.

Cell references   The system by which an item or group of items of data in a spreadsheet are referenced, e.g. A4 (column A row 4).

Clip Art   Collections of popular images and useful graphics that are made available to enhance the presentation of documents.

Control (CTRL) key   A key that is used together with another key to modify the code sent to the computer.

Copy   An operating utility command which lets you make a copy of a file onto another disk or into another subdirectory or into the same subdirectory but with a different filename.

Data   The raw facts input into the computer.

Database   An organised, structured collection of related data that is defined and processed using a database management system.

Data integrity   This refers to ensuring the correctness of the data at all stages – at point of entry, throughout processing and at output.

Data Protection Act   The legislation that exists to ensure the security and integrity of personal computer-based data.

Data security   This is concerned with ensuring that data held on a computer system can be accessed or updated only by those users who have authority.

Default   The settings that the hardware and software are set to start up with.

Delete   An operating utility command which lets you erase a file.

Desktop publishing   Software which enables the creation of artwork documents for publishing through the manipulation of text and images. Many word processing packages include DTP features whilst 'high end' DTP will produce copy ready for final printing.

Diagnostic software   Software designed to assist with fault finding.

Digitiser   An input device used for converting data in its current form into digital data which can be processed by the computer.

Directory   The information about the files stored on each disk to enable both the user and the computer operating system to locate the files on the disk – the directory will include details of the name, date and time created or updated, the location on the disk and the size of the file.

Disk   Data storage medium – see hard disk, floppy disk, CD-ROM.

Disk drive   The mechanical device that drives the disk and operates the read/write heads to access the data – referenced by a letter followed by a colon, e.g. C:\

Document   Term frequently used within a word processing package for a file which contains principally text and sometimes graphs and other images.

Electronic mail   Known as e-mail – a communication system that enables messages and information to be sent electronically to other users – it is a way of carrying out rapid, text-based communication across an organisation and potentially outside it.

Environment   This is a 'user-friendly' way of working with the computer which hides the 'raw' operating system and lets the user carry out many of the basic functions through the use of WIMPs.

Escape (Esc) key   This key is used to send a command to the computer – different packages use this key in different ways but most frequently to cancel an instruction.

Extension   The second part of a filename in MS-DOS and some other operating systems – often used to indicate the type of file.

Fax (facsimile) The transmission of exact copies of a document across the telephone network – any documents, whether hand-written or containing pictures, diagrams, graphs, charts or typed text can be transmitted at great speed for relatively low costs.

Filename Every file has a name to identify and access it – the name must be unique within the subdirectory(folder) and disk that it is stored on – each operating system has a set of rules about the structure of filenames and permitted characters.

Floppy disk A lower capacity disk, usually 1.44Mb, which is not kept permanently inside the computer but is removed when not being used.

Folder This is an alternative term for subdirectory used in many systems.

Footer The area below the main part of a page used to include text that can appear at the bottom of every page of the document and may include page numbers.

Format (noun) The way an item of data or a piece of text is presented.

Format (verb) The process of preparing a new unused disk for use with a particular operating system and disk drive.

Function keys There are usually twelve of these keys across the top of the keyboard and they are often set up to carry out commands for a particular package.

Gigabyte 1,073,741,824 bytes – often referred to as one thousand million or an American billion.

Graphics There are two types – vector and bitmap images.

Graphics tablet A flat board connected to the computer on which you can draw images with a special pen – these are displayed directly on the VDU and can be stored in the computer.

Greyscale The digital progression of density in a monochrome image.

Hard disk A high capacity disk which is usually permanently inside the computer.

Hard return The code included in a word processing document to indicate the end of a paragraph, achieved by pressing the return (also called enter) key.

Hardware The physical parts of the computer system.

Header The area above the main part of a page used to include text that can appear at the top of every page of the document and may include page numbers.

Housekeeping The management and maintenance of the disk filing system.

Icon An image which is used to represent a command or function that you wish to carry out.

ICT Information and communications technology – a term frequently replacing the term IT, to include the communication of the information by the technology to another user or computer.

Image See graphics.

Index An alphabetical list usually with section and page references – the creation of this list is often a facility available in wordprocessing packages based on marked text.

Information Processed data that has been given meaning – the output from the computer.

Ink-jet printer Output device used to produce good-quality printouts – particularly cost-effective for colour printouts.

Internet An international network of computers that makes possible the worldwide interchange of information – can be accessed through an Internet Provider.

IT Information Technology – a term used generally to describe the use of computers to capture, process and provide information.

Keyboard This is one of the main input devices, frequently including the standard QWERTY keys, a numeric keypad, cursor control keys and function keys – this type of keyboard is known as an extended or 102-key keyboard.

Kilobyte 1,024 bytes – often referred to as one thousand bytes.

Landscape The orientation of the printed document so that the paper is wider than it is long.

Laser printer Output device used to produce high quality printouts.

Licence An authority to use a piece of software – most software is supplied under some form of licence.

Light pen A pen-shaped input device which is pointed at the screen to make selections or to create images.

Megabyte 1,048,576 bytes – often referred to as one million bytes.

Memory Temporary storage areas.

Menu   A set of options (drop down or pull down) which is usually used to give you a choice from a number of similar commands or functions.

Monitor   See VDU.

Mouse   This is an input device with one, two or three buttons with a ball underneath which is moved across a flat surface to control a pointer on the screen; can also be a touch controlled device.

Network   A number of computers and peripherals connected together in order to share resources and access to data, and to provide communication facilities between users.

Newspaper columns   In word processing this refers to columns of text that flow from top to bottom and continue at the top.

Numeric keypad   Usually on the right hand side of the keyboard with numbers 0–9 and the four calculation symbols (+-*/) and an enter key – mainly used for rapid input of numeric data.

Numerical models   A defined set of rules to calculate or project numerical data – spreadsheet software is one of the most frequently used packages to achieve this.

Object   A discrete item contained within a word processing document – e.g. an imported image.

Operating system   The sets of instructions and rules that enable the different parts of the computer to work together – it will include software to start the computer, to interpret each key pressed and display it on the screen, to save the work you do and to communicate with any devices that are attached to the system, such as disk drives, printers, plotters or devices to communicate with other computers.

Orientation   The direction of the printed document – see landscape and portrait.

Package   A set of programs that can be bought 'off-the-shelf' to meet the needs of a particular application.

Paragraph   In word processing a paragraph is all the text between two hard returns – many formatting functions and particularly word wrap and justification are applied a paragraph at a time.

Parallel columns   In word processing this refers to columns of text where each block of text in a column starts on the same line as that in the column adjacent to it.

Password   A secret code entered by the user to gain access to the computer or to an area of the data and systems; used to maintain data security.

Path   The way through to a file on a disk – this path indicates the route from the directory you are currently working in within the directory tree to the subdirectory where the file is located.

Plotter   An output device used to produce high-quality graphics data – the image is created using a number of different coloured pens which are picked up and put down by an 'arm' which moves across the paper.

Pointer   Used to select an option or position on the screen – this pointer will usually be controlled through the use of an input device such as a mouse or light pen.

Portrait   The orientation of the printed document so that the paper is longer than it is wide.

Printer   An output device used to produce a permanent paper-based copy – sometimes referred to as hard copy – see laser printer and ink-jet printer.

Processor   The part of the computer that carries out the instructions.

RAM   Random access memory – the part of memory which temporarily holds the programs (instructions) you are using and the data that you are inputting – it is usually volatile, that is when you switch off the computer anything in RAM that has not been stored will be lost.

Restore   An operating utility which lets you recreate a usable copy of your files from a backup copy.

ROM   Read only memory – this is a part of memory that you can read from only, you cannot change it by adding, editing or deleting anything.

Root directory   This is the main directory set up on each disk when it is formatted – it is referenced by the use of the back slash (\).

Scanner   An input device used to capture images and text from the printed page.

Screen   See VDU.

Setup   The way the system, software and hardware, has been installed and organised to enable the user to get the best from it in terms of memory, type of printing facilities and most frequently used aspects of the packages.

Soft return   The start of a new line inserted by the software to meet the paragraph margins – it is automatically adjusted as necessary to take into account any changes to the content or layout of the paragraph.

Software Programs or sets of instructions to carry out a computer operation or application.

Sound card A circuit board which enables high quality sound to be produced on the computer – essential when using multimedia software.

Spellcheck A facility available in many packages including word processing, spreadsheets and desk top publishing to check the spelling and to offer possible corrections from a dictionary – dictionaries are often available for a number of languages.

Spreadsheet A generic package which provides a freeform tool to enable calculations and the creation of numerical models; can also represent the data in the form of charts and graphs.

Subdirectory A sub-division of a directory – the system is hierarchical and enables you to organise your files so that you can find them more easily; also known as a folder.

Systems software The software that enables the computer to work.

Table of contents This lists the main headings and subheadings for each section of a document – this list is in sequential order and will usually include page numbers – the creation of such a table of contents is often a facility available in word processing packages based on marked text.

VDU Visual display unit – the output device which enables the computer to communicate with you; both what you input and the responses from the system appear on this device – may also be referred to as a monitor or screen.

Vector graphics Images constructed using lines with precise start and end points – typically used for technical applications, as the resulting images are more precise and better able to be manipulated as objects.

Virus Piece of software which can attach itself to a storage area (disk or memory) and cause errors to occur in the operation of the computer or damage to the data.

WIMPs Stands for Windows, Icons, Menus and Pointers – the usual working environment on most computers.

Window An area on the screen which lets you view an activity – you can have more than one window open at any time and can therefore look at and work on a number of different activities at the same time.

Word processing Software which enables the creation, saving, editing and printing of documents – modern word processing facilities include not only sophisticated text manipulation and presentation functions but the facility for integration of data from other packages and the inclusion of graphical images.

Workstation The complete work space of the user – this includes not only the main parts of the computer but also the mouse mat, desk, chair, lighting, etc.

Unit Mapping Grid

Element	Intro-duction	Unit 201	Unit 204	Unit 206	Unit 208	Unit 202	Unit 203	Unit 205	Unit 207	Unit 212	Appen-dix
Mandatory units											
201.1	✓	✓		✓							
201.2	✓	✓		✓							
201.3		✓									
204.1		✓	✓	✓							
204.2			✓								
204.3			✓								
204.4			✓								
206.1				✓							
206.2				✓							
208.1			✓		✓						✓
208.2					✓						
Optional units											
202.1	✓				✓	✓					
202.2	✓				✓	✓					
202.3	✓					✓					
203.1	✓						✓				
203.2	✓				✓		✓				
203.3	✓						✓				
205.1					✓			✓			
205.2					✓			✓			
205.3	✓							✓			
207.1	✓				✓				✓		
207.2	✓				✓				✓		
207.3	✓								✓		
212.1	✓				✓					✓	
212.2	✓				✓					✓	
212.3	✓									✓	

Index

plotter 27
pointer 29
portrait 98
printers 25, 33, 35, 44, 90, 143, 145

R

RAM 22, 107
Repetitive Strain Injury *see* RSI
reports
    database 153
    layout 103
ROM 27
RSI 78

S

scanner 26
screen, *see* VDU
security 18
software
    applications 30
    database 148
    graphics 138
    licences 16
    spreadsheet 113
    word-processing 97
sort
    data 119, 152
    text 105

sound card 26
spellcheck 5
spreadsheet 31, 113
styles
    house 101
    paragraph 104

T

table of contents 111
tabulation 104
text
    copyright 17
    enhancement 100
    format 104
    manipulation 105
    processing 97

V

VDU 25, 46, 73, 76
videoconferencing 134
viruses 54
Visual Display Unit *see* VDU

W

WIMPs 28, 29
Windows 28, 46, 106
word processing 31, 97
working relationships 87